NEITHER HAY
NOR GRASS

Books by John Gould

NEW ENGLAND TOWN MEETING

PRE-NATAL CARE FOR FATHERS

FARMER TAKES A WIFE

THE HOUSE THAT JACOB BUILT

AND ONE TO GROW ON

NEITHER HAY NOR GRASS

NEITHER HAY NOR GRASS

JOHN GOULD

Down East Books

Camden, Maine

Down East Books

An imprint of The Rowman & Littlefield Publishing Group, Inc.
4501 Forbes Blvd., Ste. 200
Lanham, MD 20706
www.rowman.com

Distributed by NATIONAL BOOK NETWORK

Copyright © 2020 Estate of John Gould

British Library Cataloguing in Publication Information available

**Library of Congress Cataloging-in-Publication Data
available**

ISBN 978-1-60893-542-0 (paperback)
ISBN 978-1-60893-543-7 (e-book)

∞™ The paper used in this publication meets the minimum
requirements of American National Standard for Information
Sciences—Permanence of Paper for Printed Library Materials,
ANSI/NISO Z39.48-1992.

I DEDICATE THIS BOOK severally to the neighbors around Lisbon Ridge, who indulge me in such vagaries as these without batting an eye, and speak to me each time we meet with seeming enthusiasm, and don't seem to mind having me about so much as you might think. They make the neighborhood worth living in, in spite of me—they are gentlefolks, scholars, and good judges of pie. They never berate me about things I write, even though they read them and rightly divide the word.

—J. G.

NEITHER HAY
NOR GRASS

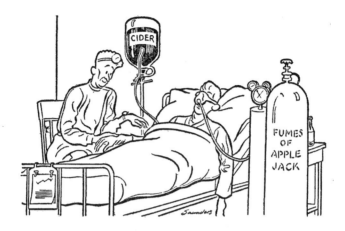

*It doesn't matter
 what you pay.*

NO DOUBT NO REMARKS OF MINE
will ever dim the mellowed fame of Benjamin
Franklin, who once admonished us not to pay too
much for our whistles. Mr. Franklin was a practical man and he had a practical man's regard for
whistles. To him a whistle was so much material
outlay, so much manufacturing time, a bit of ingenuity, and some wind. To him, with this inven-
tory, he could compute whistles at ten cents a
gross, or in his own time at not above a shilling
the shoal.

I am in love with practicality as much as any
man, but all in its proper place and time—there
are moments when practicality is a sin. According

13

to my most impractical estimate of a whistle, Ben Franklin was all wrong. I have the whimsical notion that there isn't enough money in the world to weigh off the kind of a whistle I made today. What this does to the reputation of old Mr. F., I don't care.

It is spring. The winter rye is growing by inches, and the pussy willows are turned to leaves. The first Bob-o-link and the first oriole have saluted us. One of the hens seemed to have a happy thought and started clucking. The apple buds are in tight pink clusters. It is whistle weather.

Once in a man's whole lifetime does the true and perfect whistle weather come. It isn't when he's a boy, as I used to think, and he has his first spring whistle. It's when he's a man, and has a boy of his own to make a whistle for. With me, it was when we were four-and-a-half, with spring at the morn and the Balm o' Gilead heavy on the air. We really didn't have a whistle in mind, but had just started out for a walk to be amazed at anything we found worthy of our attention.

To make a proper whistle, a man has to start out from the house with his boy by the hand, stopping first at the pond to watch the peepers scurry for cover in the deeper part. You begin with a labored explanation of how the peepers live in stone walls all year, but go into the ponds in the spring so they can lay their eggs. If you're real agile, you can snatch one before he jumps, and show him off—a tiny frog with suction cups on his fingers and the true cross of Jesus on his back. Frogs have to lay their eggs in water, and this is a frog, and here he is.

"Like hen's eggs, Daddy?"

And the walk goes on past the beehives, where a few bees are flying in with pollen all yellow on their whiskery legs. Then a first shoot of asparagus is found, the first leaves on the raspberries. A fence post has hove loose with the winter frost, and we prop it back with a rock until we can really fix it.

"Can the cow jump that high?"

Over the fence some ferns poked their fiddleheads up, and I found a boxberry plum. Spring boxberry plums are dry as dry, but their dainty checkerberry flavor is something any boy wants to know about. His fist shut up on three or four fat ones to be manhandled until he could get them home to Mother.

The violets and trillium could wait until we were coming back, and then they could be picked, too, for Mummy. I tried to explain that lovely ladies like violets, but that a true country gentleman thought twice before he took his fair one a mess of trillium.

"I think she'd like them if I picked them."

The ensuing explanation gave him the joyful acquisition of "stinking benjamin" as a proper

15

word for his rural vocabulary. He made good use of it for a couple of weeks.

A crow, a fat spring crow, had been dozing on a pine and got caught unawares. He gave a squawk and dropped behind the tree so we couldn't see him fly away. And not a detail of this fine spring morning was any different from another spring morning I had remembered from thirty years before. It seemed long ago until that morning, but now it was all one and the same day. So recent that the two mornings had no identity apart from each other, and I was both father and son, all at once. I knew just what to do next, to say next.

The thing to do, of course, was make a whistle. We had to scout down by the swamp and find a willow shoot, and the rest was just knife work. A rolling cut with the small blade of the knife, and a good twist to bring off the bark. Smaller eyes are watching, and thirty years later, or so, they will remember all this. A fellow has to be good in the eyes of his son, and there mustn't be any unprofessional maneuver. But it doesn't take long to make a whistle, even if Daddy isn't too deft. The smooth willow wood is notched for the air chamber, a passage made for blowing, and a handy if mussed boxberry plum dropped in to provide a pea. Then the wood is wet in the mouth —highly unsanitary in every respect—and the carefully kept bark pushed back into its original place.

Now all you need is a little boy who can puff out his cheeks and blow, and you get a screech well worth the trouble. You also get two small eyes that sparkle and shine until you begin to get the idea being a Daddy isn't the worst thing in the world.

The whistle, naturally, proves beyond the shadow of a doubt that Daddy is the smartest and best and finest and most wonderful man in the whole world. Many men work hard to become revered by their fellows, but a simple willow whistle will confuse them all and leave Daddy head and shoulders over everybody else—even Benjamin Franklin. The spring whistle has more than magic in it, Wisdom herself couldn't be so wise in the ways of men and boys and the time of the year. I watch him blow his soul into each toot, and anybody could see that the things a willow whistle means and does are safe in the continuity of time. Three decades hence—well, there but for the space of time go I.

We have to take our things home and show Mummy. Mummy accepts the boxberry plums, the tight wad of violets—even the stinking benjamin, just one. But the whistle is the thing. The top of her head almost flies off in the kitchen as the whistle speaks its springtime wonder and cheeks are puffed out beyond belief. "Wasn't Daddy nice?" she says, and there's nothing to be gained by wondering just what she meant.

Because Mummy is a mummy-dear, and couldn't ever really understand things like men and boys and whistles. Like Benjamin Franklin, who was very practical, she wouldn't ever know that once in a man's life a willow whistle is beyond any price at all.

❀ ❀ ❀

Everybody thinks
it's very funny.

THE GENERAL SUBJECT OF GOING to hell continues to occupy many minds, and the evils of strong drink have much attention. Personally, I am not a drunkard, and scarcely any of my time is spent in bacchanalian revelries or debauch. Even if I were so inclined, I would not look upon the wine when it is red on account of the heavy taxes. And I am not beguiled by the modern political husbandry that looks upon intoxication as a public service, on account of how the welfare department and old age assistance are financed by the drinking masses. Looking cross-eyed at a revenue stamp on the neck of a bottle is not my idea of honoring Father and Mother.

What I do is make cider. This is a home industry and thus far it has not been controlled and taxed by the government. I don't know why it hasn't, and I haven't inquired. I'm not going to remind anybody.

18

Cider, as an explosive, is wholly a passing phase. In its beginning and its end cider is a harmless item used by the most violent temperance devotees with impunity. The alpha and omega stages should be disposed of before considering the interim:

In the fall of the year the apples are gathered from the orchards in all their luscious beauty. It is my good fortune to have a young man with a Boy Scout belt and a young lady with pigtails to help me. The boy and I are interested in the better grades and we carefully collect and sort the crop. The young lady is the cider expert. Her job is to pick up the drops and arrange them in the front of the big trailer that follows our farm tractor up the orchard rows. In due time we arrive at the grading place and the boxes are disposed—some for roadside sale, some for the markets, some for the dark recesses of the concrete apple cellar where they will mellow for winter use and sale. Then, before each return trip to the orchards we bag the ciders our young lady has piled up front. In due time the pile of bags is impressive, and we go to the cider mill.

Cider apples are not a loss—they fetch a fair price from processors who make apple juice, sweet cider in jugs, jellies, pectin and vinegar. They can be sold to men who distill apple brandy. So the cider brought home by the orchardist for his own use is hardly more than a by-product.

This year I made three 60-gallon barrels of by-product.

We loaded the empty barrels into the truck first, piled in the bags of apples, and the three of us struck out. The grinders ceased not until the last big Golden Russet was chewed to shreds, and the hydraulic press had squeezed from it the last iota of juice. The young lady stood beside the dripping press and drank from a tin dipper—thus incurring a digestive disturbance that ran better than a week and was not helped any by subsequent libations. The lad waited his turn, and then I had some. Only those who have drunk deep from the cider-press's immediate product have any notion of the magnificent delight attendant. Now the cider is sweet-sweet. The vegetable ferments have not yet girded their loins or lifted their clear clarion cries. The National President of the Woman's Christian Temperance Union could imbibe publicly at this time with profit to herself and honor to her position. Any suggestion that cider, on pressing day, is allied in any way to the more muscular brands of potables is utter idiocy. It is the beverage of Sunday Schools at Halloween, the refreshment of polite ladies' clubs, the joy of the abstemious. Delicious beyond compare, sweet cider is a fine thing and nobody can say it nay.

In this condition we bring it home. It is horsed up in its barrels in the cool cellar. The upper bungs are banged out so the children can insert straws and enjoy a brief pleasure. Brief—because when the bungs come out the living air goes in, and the enzymes perk up and flex their biceps and grab holt. A barrel of cider, working for you in the cellar, is not a creature of the welfare state. It knoweth not the clock and whistle; it puts in a full 36-hour day; and it chargeth not for overtime. By the following Tuesday the open bung on the top of a barrel is a cluster of seething foam and chum, and the cellar has a new and interesting aroma. The children, now, are standing back and show respect. So let us pass now from the beginnings even unto the end, which is vinegar.

A couple of years later the lady will have assembled in the kitchen a variety of garden items. There are cucumbers, young onions, dill, tomatoes, peppers, cauliflower, green beans, and other things at other times in other kitchens. It is the pickle season. From under the sinkshelf she will bring forth a gallon jug, string looped through the handle, and she will say, "Dear, want to get me some vinegar?"

Then ariseth the stalwart man of the house, and he takes the jug and he descends into the cellar by a well-worn stair. He goes to his barrels, and he thumps this one and that one, and at length he draws off a jugful from the barrel of his choice. The cellar, once again, is filled with an aroma—this time it is rich, cutting, breathtaking. This is none of your self-service, supermarket vinegar, diluted to an average 28%. There is no minimum standard here. This vinegar will wound at fifty yards, and kill at ten. It has an edge like a samurai sword, and a velocity no physicist has yet reduced to formula. It is the real McCoy —cider vinegar that has meditated quietly for a long time and has convinced itself on every point. A good vinegar maker contrives to keep his manufactures on a rotating schedule, so not all the barrels are vinegar and not all of them are sweet cider. He comes up to the kitchen, wiping his mouth, and the wife goes ahead with the pickles —shortly the house is redolent of spices and vinegar and hot pickle syrup, God is Great and God is Good, and the whole big wide wonderful world is a magnificent idea. Life goes on, but the vinegar has fulfilled its destiny—the apple drops in the orchard have gone from hither to hence, and the great ultimate achievement has been attained. If you want something nice, just spread about an inch of that piccalilli on a plate of hot baked beans and motion everybody to close the door.

We are now about to consider the meantime —the months and years when the barrels have ceased to be sweet cider and have not yet acetified. We should approach our study objectively, and strive to maintain a clinical attitude. I deplore

22

the facetious remarks of uninformed folks who jest about cider—they never felt a wound. They think it is something funny, like whiskey or rum, and there are even people who say it is practically the same thing as champagne. They will stop on the street and say, "How is your cider coming along, hee hee?" They seem to think cider is for amusement, and that anybody who makes any should be inviting company all the time. Personally, as a maker of good cider in my own cellar, I have always avoided any social contacts which might result in my being invited into another cider maker's cellar. I have also refrained from letting people pot at me with .30-30 rifles. I remain dignified in the presence of cider, and remove my hat when it is mentioned, and treat it with respect. I do not intrude my presence upon it. I do not give it a chance to strike first. I would be the last to suggest that cider be used for entertainment purposes, or as a social beverage. And yet I find many people who think that is why I make cider.

In referring to my notes here, I find that the alcoholic content of cider is not high, as compared to distilled or fortified liquors. It runs about the same as any fermented fruit juice, and even when doctored by experimental folks it refrains from building up anything to alarm the chemists. Instead, cider is low in alcohol, but high in the vitamins and proteins. It has a short cream line, but a high score. A home economics teacher who tested mine for virulency said it was the carbohydrates, and reported that it didn't give her a headache in the winter any worse than it did in the summer. She said the fatty globules coagulate almost at once with the lymphatic secretions, thus setting up a super-balance in the blood stream, whereupon the minute particles of alcohol infiltrate and appear magnified. It is much like a number of dwarfs in a crowd, but with clubs. The effect is like hitting a baked custard with a canoe paddle. The patient is carried away with an internal exuberance that arises not from the alcohol, but from his own system's failure to adjust chemically to the dawn of a new era.

The protein content of interim cider has had definite recognition as an antidote for the common cold. Upon the first evidence of a scratchy throat or tightening membranes, cider should be applied liberally. This will clear up a cold faster than any other known remedy as prescribed by specialists. One man who took cider to cure a cold awoke to find himself in perfect health, and his physician told him he had been miraculously cured by nothing more than the cider. The man had also had pleurisy, pneumonia, ruptured appendix, sciatica, measles and whooping cough in the meantime, and knew nothing whatever about any of them. Cider would have more widespread

24

prescribing from the medical profession if it were more generally available, but nowadays most physicians scarcely know where to get enough for themselves. I know this is so because my physician has told me so, hee hee.

As I stated in the beginning, I am not a drinking man. I cannot afford to take stimulants under our current revenue code, and I have not been able to bring myself to a drunkard's end to support the old age pension plan. Nor have I mastered courage enough to become a cider fiend. I endure the jibes of my uninformed friends only because ultimately we will need some vinegar. And also because the common cold is a constant threat and I wish to be protected at all times. I am unusually healthy, and have not had a cold now for many years, other than slight touches about three times a week.

The only other use I have for my barrels down cellar is to go down and admire them as a potent beverage in a well-regulated field of taxation, on which no legislature has yet levied a revenue of $10 a gallon. I don't see how they could do it without making pickles a crime.

❦ ❦ ❦

I think we've got
some good ideas.

SPEAKING OF THE VAST SUBJECT
of modern, or ram-rodded, Education (with a
capital E) it occurs to me that a lot of people
may not know about beaver ponds, and planting
sweet peas, and what you do for corn meal, which,
with the wind in the south, presents a situation
we have just met head-on and subdued.

I don't know why, but a lot of people don't
seem to do too well with sweet peas. I take a
wheelbarrow about this time of year and push
it down under the barn and fill it up, and then
I push it up to the dooryard and work it in good
around the edge of the flower garden. Then I toss
down a couple of ounces of sweet pea seed and
forget about them. Along in the season we have
millions of sweet peas and everybody says, "Oh,
tell me how you do it." Well, I've just told you
how I do it.

Some of our flowers get a lot more attention
and never seem to do so well. But with sweet
peas I'm a dabster. I heap the wheelbarrow up
good, and if that makes a difference I wouldn't
be surprised. Farm experts have studied long and
tirelessly, but they've never found a better way to
farm than to have a wheelbarrow well loaded at
the right time. So I spaded up for my sweet peas
and planted them, and the lad helped me. He
26

observed that every time I turned over a forkful of the rich soil a number of gorgeous great angleworms were revealed. By the time the sweet pea seed was covered these worms came about two-thirds of the way up the can. And by the rarest fortuitousness the wind that balmy spring evening was hugging into the south so you wouldn't believe it, and things looked most favorable. Most favorable, indeed.

At this time I should like to make it clear that the lad and I have a working arrangement which appears to be turning out 100%. I am not the world's greatest advocate of what the professional Educators refer to as Centralized Schooling—not for our part of the country. The idea came about in the greater stretches of the west'ard sections, and applying it to Maine is an intellectual absurdity unworthy of our breed. The lad takes a miserable beating, and it isn't fair. He gets up in the morning to do his chores and have his breakfast, and stands out by the mailbox before eight o'clock to catch the school bus. This wonderful modern convenience carries him two miles to the village to school. The wicked, nasty, old, dark-ages rural school that he thus avoids is a short walk up the road, and a great and wonderful age which has showered every convenience and gadget on the remote farm home has done nothing to make the rural school modern. Within months a great and wise Educator arose and made sneering remarks about the open privies in rural schools, leading his remarks into the conclusion that rural schools are a curse. Evidently the fatheads who make such speeches don't know that you can have running water, electric lights, automatic oil heat, and anything else you want out in the country. If rural schools, today, still have open privies it is only because professional Educators are too ignorant to embrace modern progress. Here in this town they are operating crowded, dingy, unhealthy village schools that actually are worse than the rural schools as they now stand. Their argument that teachers, good teachers, won't take rural schools is also predicated on the old-times. If some school superintendent would fix up an old-time rural school, putting in all the conveniences now available, I think they'd be surprised how many good teachers would gladly swap crowded village conditions for a chance to move out where there's air, sunshine, birds that sing, and good hearty country people to take an interest in what they do. But they continue to plead for funds to enlarge village facilities, and refuse to leave country children to adorn their inquiring minds out in the country where they belong and where they are better off. Today the village children walk to school, and our hearty farm youngsters are muscle-bound from riding bus seats.

There's more to it than that. They also have a

hot lunch program, and it took our lad less than a week to figure that out. With his 20¢ a day he was quickly surfeited on spaghetti and meat scraps, and he found that the approved, five-star, government-recommended snack was no substitute for mother's cooking. He put up a clamor for dinner in an old-fashioned lunchbucket. There was, to be sure, some snide insinuations about our not supporting the semi-sacred institution of subsidized edibles, but it didn't work. The lad agrees with me that his mother runs the best boarding house in town, and that surplus commodities steeped in the political juice of a welfare state are a damned poor substitute for something to eat. He said as much, so we let him carry his lunch. So he goes to his labors, and he returns on the bus about 3.30 or 4.00 in the afternoon. This is a long day in the mines, and laboring men have organized unions to spare themselves the equivalent. Now that the lad is older, he takes it better, but the ordeal begins at six and is difficult to take at that age. Citizens who remonstrate at the fantastic Educational program are put in their places by the reminder that the professionals know best. There's a lot more to it than this, and I realize a good part of it is localized, but the point is that Friday comes around and finds my laddie in a bad state of schoolhouse dithers. He is exhausted —jumpy and irritable. So I set up a counter-program and designed my week ends so the lad and

29

I could figure out things to do to get him ready for the next exhausting week. That's about where we were when we found our tin can amazingly full of sleek, fat angleworms fresh from nature's abundant hatchery.

Now, it so happened, that balmy evening, that I thought up an errand at Webster Corner—some little thing I have since forgotten—and by the most unfortunate mischance the man I went to see didn't happen to be home. It came to me at once that he hadn't made his home there since the place burned in 1922. So the lad and I were at Webster Corner with a can of worms and not a single thing to do there. So we put our heads together and thought we might as well.

Strangely enough, there chanced to be a brook near by, and we had somehow parked our automobile so it was just a step through the woods. Sometimes these things happen so advantageously that collusion is suspected. We were so infinitely lucky that we hit this brook right where a colony of industrious beavers had labored hard. They had labored so well that they had backed up water over about a hundred acres of woodland, creating a pond from which the living trees still rose in profusion. Now when beavers do that, the trout are delighted, and soon afterward they appear behind the dam and fructify and abound until their numbers and size surpass belief. The nature of a beaver pond is such that an angler can't get near it on account of the water, and people who fish a good brook generally pass by on high ground when they come to a beaver pond. People who do that are foolish. It was my intention to show the lad how an honest and industrious fisherman, willing to wet his feet up to his armpits, could come home assured that the game is well worth the candle.

The schoolroom is no place to learn that, and I suppose it's true that the millions we've spent on Education have never yet produced an angler. So the lad and I crept through the brake and puckerbrush, now and then falling flat in the brackish water, and by much striving we found ourselves far out in the beaver pond where the foot of Walton hadn't trod since the beavers raised the level. The lad said it looked like a good place.

To confirm his observation a smacking great trout went ker-choonk a few feet ahead of him, indicating a spot where a mayfly had recently emerged. The lad avoided a popple on the right, a cedar to the left, and successfully inserted an angleworm directly on the ring of ripples spreading from the location. Nobody but a trout fisherman will understand how short a time was involved between the arrival of the angleworm and the hooking of the trout.

Being a good angler and a good father, it was my duty to appear not to notice the excitement that followed. I laboriously inspected my own angleworm, made as if testing my line, looked about to see if there were any bluebirds in the vicinity, and said I guessed I'd light my pipe. All this time the splashing sounded like an aluminum canoe beating into a chop, and the lad eventually wound up back on high ground, in a clump of junipers, holding the trout in a death clutch and reporting he was certainly long enough to keep. He certainly was—by seven good inches and some to spare, and if he wouldn't go a pound it was too slight a difference to worry about.

He joined me again, water to his chest, and we shortly took thirteen trout before dusk set in and we had to feel slowly back through the popples and driki to dry land. We had a canvas to spread under our wet seats, and we got into the automobile and drove home.

"Didn't we do well?" he asked, and it appeared to me that his observation smacked of accuracy. When we got home we told Mother that the man up to Webster Corner wasn't living there now, but we didn't fool her any. She said, "I haven't a speck of corn meal in the house." So we had to use cracker crumbs, and with the spider full of deep salt pork fat they seemed to work all right. A family of four can have a lot of fun with thirteen trout.

After the lad got in bed that night, cheeks rosy and eyes bright, I went up and tossled his head and he said, "We ought to plant sweet peas more often."

But that's the way our week-end homework goes. A school can never match what nature teaches for free. There's no point in teaching youngsters to count unless they have something to count. I don't have a synopsis from any state department, and I am far from accredited. And I don't lie awake nights thinking up some way to get a percentage increase in salary. I just grab the week-end's opportunity and make the most of it. I'd get crotchety under classroom routine, too, but out here on the farm I notice that routine is the last thing we depend on. Our teaching goes on whether a building is open or not. And best of all, the teacher learns at least as much as the pupil.

I won't say that my technique finds me always ready, but that is because I am an amateur, and don't appreciate the subtler nuances. As with the ice cream. The best part of the ice cream lesson is that you can do it in hot weather after schools close in June. We were setting out a bed of late onions on this occasion, and our conversations were such that I was neglecting my role of teacher. These were Ebenezer onions. They used to call them Japanese onions, but the war came along and things that were Japanese lost favor. That fall the seedsmen had all ordered Japanese onions, but when they came in the spring they were billed as Ebenezers. They were the same onion, but like all of us they had conformed to total war. I was telling him how Hamburger steaks became Victory steaks back when I was a boy, for about the same reason, and he said, "I guess I like working in the garden best, after all."

I said, "After all what?"

"After all nothing. I thought I liked it third."

I said, "Your father is a doddering old dolt, and his mind no longer functions with its pristine vigor. What are you talking about?"

"Our reading survey."

"In school?"

"Sure."

"What about it?"

"Well, I said I liked working in the garden third."

"Which undoubtedly has something to do with reading."

We didn't get anywhere, and after a while we got the onions lined up and went to the house for supper. He got out his survey and showed me. The first question asked how many books he had read since Christmas. His answer was seven, but the survey didn't ask and he didn't remember what they were. He did read some books, I know that, but the only one I recalled was *Joe Strong, The Boy Fish.* The next answer said he had five magazines he read regularly, and I think that's pretty good. It's five more than I read. He also said he

34

read newspapers regularly, with special attention to world news, editorials, pictures, headlines and advertisements. Jokes and comics, he said, were not perused. At that time Joe Palooka was in great distress, and I assume that a boy of tender years might not readily identify that strip as a comic. I didn't argue.

So this reading survey went. He said he read comic books, and had mastered sixteen since Christmas. Actually he has never shown any interest in them, which pleases his mother and me, and as far as close study goes he's never seen but one. That was a Dick Tracy that was left in our outhouse up in the woods at the sugar camp by a man I hired to chop some wood. I left it on the seat after I noticed it was drawn by a man named Gould. We had a relative who left here years back under an odium stimulated by the girl's mother, and his descendants keep popping up. During maple sugar season the book had a daily workout, and I happen to know he read it. We all did. There wasn't anything else to read. But I asked him where he got the figure sixteen.

"I guess I meant six."

"Well, where did you get six?"

"All the kids read them."

"That's all right—you can read them too, if you want to. But I didn't think you cared about them."

"I don't, but you see—you're supposed to put down answers the teachers expect."

Maybe so, maybe so. Then we came to the part where he listed his likes and dislikes. First, he liked to write letters to friends, next to go to a party, and third to work in the garden. Last of all, he disliked to wash dishes. It may be hard for urban Educators to realize that we have had an electric dishwasher in our remote and bucolic home for years, and that Mother has never asked her doting son to touch a wiper, but it is true, and I suspect his answer was also to beguile, somehow, his teacher. I said I'd like to give a survey to people who make surveys, and then we came to the ice cream. He had written "Yes" where it asked if he would like to read so he could write an article about making ice cream.

I said, "Why don't you write an article on planting onions?"

He said, "I don't have to read to do that."

I said, "That's what I'm coming at. Why don't we make some ice cream so you can write about it without reading?"

So we went out and dug for a piece of ice and got the old freezer from the shed attic. We shaved off what ice we'd need, and Mother helped him mix the ingredients. We decided on vanilla for a starter, and he is planning to do an article on it shortly. I outdistanced him on the third dish, and also on the article—but it is a wise teacher who keeps ahead of the pupil.

The abundant opportunity to direct the boy

underfoot is constantly amazing. I find there is no difficulty at all in "awakening interest." His unbounded enthusiasm for every moment makes me wonder about these teachers who can't seem to keep a class alert. A while ago I had a man here helping me make some finish lumber in the shop. The lad stepped up and began pulling strips away from the power saw. Immediately the saw bound, the motor ran hot, and the thermal switch shut everything off. So while it cooled the man gave the lad a beautiful lesson that no professional teacher could have equaled. He explained about the set of a saw, how the kerf mustn't be pinched against the blade. Then, a few words about how a wise sawyer never reaches in over the table and thus retains his fingers into his advanced senility. I suppose the schools have safety instruction—they must have. But I'm not worrying about the lad and power tools. He knows. He knows why old Lars Swensen has only two fingers on one hand, and he knows it from Lars himself.

It's easy for a man to say, "Now stand back, Sonny, you'll only get hurt." But it's just as easy to keep the boy working with you. The good instructor says, "I wonder would you help me here a minute?" The boy leaps to assist, and holds the other end of the board with every ounce of his strength and enthusiasm. The other end of the board may not need holding, but the boy will hold it until his eyes bug out and he is a participant in the skill and artistry of a good workman. I had a plumber working here, and shortly the plumber had the lad dangling a string down a hole. This was supposed to help the plumber in some strange way, and the lad picked up quite a bit about plumbing, but the plumber was elderly and forgetful, and he forgot about the boy after a while and went home. I wound up the string in a few minutes, and gathered that the lad knew as much about pipe fitting as I ever did, and at a much earlier age.

Another carpenter we had set the lad to making a birdhouse. At going wages the birdhouse cost me a lot of money because the carpenter did the thing up right. It sounded strange to hear the child talking about male and female joints after that, but he knew which was which. The birdhouse was tongued and grooved, mortised, shiplapped and put together with the best construction throughout. The lad found out what each tool was for, and every piece was sandpapered down to the last whisper before the carpenter would allow it to be fitted. It was just about time for the Audubon era to set in, so I was glad, and I helped put the birdhouse up before the spring migration.

He caught a pair of bluebirds almost at once, and excitement ran high. They carted in string for a day or so, and then the old man bluebird sat on the roof and looked happy. The bluebirds sang a good deal, and the whole proposition seemed good until one day I saw a tree swallow dive-bomb the bluebird house, and I knew we were in for trouble.

The lad soon reported that some birds were fighting his bluebirds. I said yes, they were tree swallows, and in time they would drive the bluebirds away. I lost my Audubon button long since, and things that eventuate among the birds no longer amaze me. His button was new and shiny and he was disgusted with me. I implied, he felt, that I was going to stand idly by and let the bluebirds be persecuted. He deplored my attitude and said this was a crisis. He said I had to stop them. So we went out to view the conflict at close range and I tried to justify the ways of birds and keep within the Audubon specifications. It was quite some task. I tried to point out that tree swallows, too, are nice to have around, that they perform a definite part in the pattern of things, that you can get to like them, and that maybe bluebirds are over-rated merely because they sing prettier and have a brighter over-coat.

"But the bluebirds were here first."

"And the Indians were here when the white men came."

"What?"

"I mean that being first isn't always the thing to go by."

"It ought to be."

"I know, but nobody ever told the swallows. They don't know that. There's always somebody butts in who doesn't know the rules. The swallows think they're doing the right thing. Maybe they are."

I was going to say something about manifest destiny, and the Monroe Doctrine, and a few other things that came to mind, but I felt the matter was already complicated enough. Besides, I wasn't too sure myself. "You know," I said, "sometimes it's better to move to a nicer neighborhood. The bluebird can't fight so well, but he's smart. He'll move out. The swallows are smart, too, because they know he will. Everybody is smart, and in the end there's no harm done. Before the summer is over everybody will be happy about it."

"Not me, I want bluebirds."

"But Audubon liked all the birds. He knew swallows could drive out bluebirds, but he painted swallows one day and painted bluebirds the next and got along with both of them. He probably thought birds were a lot like some people he knew. You'll find some people you can't get along with before you get through, and these bluebirds will teach you to pick up your marbles and move somewhere else. Even if you were there first."

"If I build a house for the swallows will they let my bluebirds alone?"

"Probably not, but some people think it's worth trying. Why don't you make a lot of houses, and

40

maybe next year you will catch some bluebirds you can keep."

He's going to be a lot older, of course, before he knows that I wasn't talking so much about bluebirds and swallows at all. He made birdhouses all summer, and since then we have had bluebirds that stayed. But mostly the swallows moved in and hatched their broods, and they are kind of fun, too.

So the learning process seems to go on, and between us I think we improve every week end. I don't know why we shouldn't, there's every reason to.

*It's the most
amazing thing.*

EVERY EASTER YOU CAN BUY TEN-
cent ducks and chickens in the stores, and I've
often wondered what becomes of them in after
times. I would imagine few of them go to farm
children, because at that time of year brooder
houses are peeping and the season's work is under
way. A youngster who is lugging water to a few
hundred feathered commodities isn't going to go
to pieces over a cunning little ball of fluff that
Aunt Carrie brings home from the store. I don't
know if they put these ducklings and chicks in a
paper bag or tie them around with paper and
string, but every year plenty of them get sold

43

over the counter to children, or to the parents of children.

Well, I've found out what this arrangement is good for. I had some ducks. White Pekings. Very pretty. I got them to adorn the little pond we scooped in the area behind the barn, for fire protection. I've always had some mallards around, which are a domesticated wild bird, but I was sold the idea of having some nice white ducks by a man who was overstocked, and we added a few Pekings to beautify the surroundings. Those of the feminine persuasion were already laying eggs, and they were good at it. The boss duck supervised the industry carefully and reported production to me every morning. He was very friendly, and I could see he was on my side. The lady ducks quacked very well, but he had a lesser quack, as if he had a stick in his throat, and he would run around and tell me all about it. Every morning when I went to the pen he would line the ducks up for inspection, and then he would walk over to the nest and count the eggs for me. Then he would turn around and tell the ducks all about it, and they would remonstrate with him and make quite a to-do. When one of the ducks got caught short and wasn't able to reach the nest in time, he would mark the place in his retentive memory, and next morning would lead me over into the corner and find it. There were times when he seemed to try to single out the duck which had been so careless, but I felt this was none of my business and I didn't take any action on it. Anyway, we got to be real friends. As head mechanic he was a good man.

After the springtime warmed up I would open the sliding door, and he'd push the ducks out through and lead them up to the pond for relaxation and refreshment. This was such a knowing duck that if I chanced to open the door first he wouldn't permit the ladies to leave until I had gathered the eggs and made my customary speech of acceptance. The hens were much taken with this, and would peep through the wire into the duck pen and talk about it. The drake was a great pal, but his ducks remained impersonal and I never felt that I really got to know them well. About that time he told me one morning that the great annual incubation period had caught up with us, and for a time the morning roll call found this duck or that duck absent for cause. It takes four weeks for a duck to bring forth ducklings, and the drake and I began looking forward to this accouchement. He, alas, was not spared to witness it.

A neighbor's dog cut my drake down in his jubilant youth. He was caught between the barn and the henhouse, sort of, and that was that. The neighbor was penitent, but I could see that he didn't regard a drake as an asset of irreparable worth, and he was more or less right. I said, "Well,

I know where I can get a Peking drake to finish out the season," and we dismissed the subject. I did know, too.

The previous Easter an Aunt Carrie, or somebody, had bought a ten-cent-store duckling for Margaret Clark, a youngster down the road a step, and Margaret had made a pet of this foundling. For a time it was cute and darling, but then he got bigger and he would come into the house and climb up on the piano. A thousand times Margaret's mother threatened to wring its fool neck, and a thousand times Margaret's father stumbled over it on the way to bed and said he was going to give it away. But Margaret put up a fuss as many times, and the drake stayed on. Even when he developed his curled-up tail feathers and people knew he was a drake and he got rooty, Margaret still loved him and let him bite her fingers with his bill. This developed a little habit of going around biting the ankles of anybody who chanced by, whether he had been introduced to them or not, and many a caller on the pleasant Clark family ended up on the chopping block with Drakie jumping up and down below. As the drake's first year wore along he became a nasty little devil, and while Margaret still loved him he didn't have another friend in the world.

He was, however, a drake of the same category as my widowed ducks, and I went down to see

Margaret and see if we couldn't strike a bargain for the remainder of the mating season. I took her down a setting of eggs and told her to put them under a hot hen and in four weeks she'd have a whole lot of ducks. Her mother and father have been hardly civil to me since, and I don't blame them, but Margaret was properly impressed and I brought Drakie back to gladden the hearts of my bereft flock.

Now, from here on it's sad. This department-store duck didn't know what a pond is. Worse than that—far worse than that—he didn't even know what a duck is. I set him down by the pond, where several of his new wives were gaily playing bottoms-up and enhancing the scene in every way. He ignored both the water and the wives, and came up to me and pinched my ankles. I pushed him into the water, and he came right out again with his features contorted by unconcealed fear. I told him how foolish he was, but he paid no attention. He made the little noise with a stick in his throat and followed me back to the house and sat on the doorstep. He sits on the doorstep all the time, unless we go away, and then he goes out and sits by the R.F.D. box and twists his neck until we come back. From the pond come joyful noises of merry ducks cajoling. He heedeth not. All he wants is somebody to walk by so he can fall in and keep step. At night when I put in the ducks he looks the other way and then comes up and sits on the doorstep. He thinks he's people, just like anybody else. Foster-son to the notion counter, and Easter-duckling foundling—out of whack and emotionally unbalanced.

I would not want to be a ten-cent duck.

❦ ❦ ❦

These are the Conditions
that prevail.

WE HAVE A RIVER THAT goes by here, and it stinks. You can smell it for miles, and on a good day it will peel paint off buildings and create a rich, purple effluvia which makes everybody sad. Now and then some enthusiastic politician will arise in a rally and promise to do something about it, but shortly thereafter some eminent men convince him that he really doesn't smell anything.

I am speaking of the Androscoggin River.

People who live along the Androscoggin continue to observe its stout aroma, and observe the paint peeling off, but on every hand we are being reminded by great and good people that we are mistaken. A man at Brunswick put river water on his vegetables during a dry growing-season last summer, and produced a cucumber he couldn't lift, but simultaneously the newspapers printed statements from great industrialists that the river was really quite clean.

I don't always understand such things. There must be something in the settled life I lead which reveals basic truths to me, and makes me leery of promulgated fallacies. I can read stories about the purity of our river, and then I can go out and lean against the stench and smell it just the same. It may be that I haven't advanced, culturally, to the point where I can ignore my nose and smell only what is rationalized for me by helpful others.

The program to make us overlook the fetid zephyrs has been interesting to watch, and sometimes smelled worse than the river.

The Androscoggin rises in the lovely Rangeley Lakes, the prettiest region in the United States, and immediately flows out of Maine into New Hampshire. At this point you can dip your cup anywhere and drink without the slightest fear. Fierce landlocked salmon will rise to your fly and give you the greatest thrill now left to effete mankind. Square-tailed trout, too. It is beautiful. Then, a few miles downstream at Berlin, one of the largest paper and pulp mills in the country squats by the water-power privilege and exuberates its coffee-like redolence in all directions. Shortly thereafter the river returns to Maine and comes down a long valley to the sea. Among other places, it touches Rumford, Livermore Falls, and the twin cities of Auburn-Lewiston—each with its populations and its mills. Ten miles below it cascades over ancient ledges and opens its pores so I can smell it three miles away on my hill. It smells like paper mills and the effluvia of cities, and stagnation and death.

It wasn't too long ago that an ancestor of mine settled up here because he liked the valley. Sea-run fish crowded the river below the falls—salmon, trout, alewives, shad, sturgeon, and many another that fought up and up to the ancient spawning beds. Boys stripped and took August dips in the cool, clean water. Then they'd dress and bring a mess of trout home for supper.

But in a generation every possible insult had been perpetrated against the created loveliness of God. Forests that controlled the headwaters had been stripped away. Sawmills cast slabs, sawdust and shavings into the stream. Pulp mills found they could peel wood by letting it churn together in the spring run-off, and the clean bottoms where trout had spawned since glacial times were a rotting filth of shredded bark. Just below Brunswick accumulating debris actually built up an island— some of it eroded silt, but mostly slabs and bark and sawdust.

The cities, of course, cast their sewage into the Androscoggin—but that isn't so bad as some might think. A normal river will cleanse itself as it flows, and sewage alone will not kill off all the fish. It was the mill waste that combined with sewage—

sulphide brine and dyes and other chemical cast-offs. With its chemical balance destroyed, the river could no longer cleanse itself, and fish and vegetation simply gave up. The Androscoggin became a dead river—the water could no longer suspend sufficient oxygen.

Now, just above Lewiston a power company impounds water for its hydroelectric wheels. The power companies don't put waste and filth in rivers, but they have other ways to join in the manufacture of stink. They control flowage, and behind their dam the cultch in the river found a place to settle and congregate. This has been explained with large words in court, and judges who didn't understand it nodded sagely. In simple, unlegal, terms it seems the cultch ferments under water like brewer's yeast. Now and then it reaches a certain stage and becomes volatile. It then rises to the surface and gives off in all directions with vigor and enthusiasm. After each resurrection contact with the air changes the chemical properties so the mass sinks to the bottom again; thus fermenting again to rise again to sink again, and so on. To employ a euphemism, the river thus belches, and the power company makes kilowatts between poops. I have refrained from employing technical language, and hope I have made it clear.

Well, for a number of years the government of Maine has been carefully identified with kilowatts, pulp and paper, and associated industries, and we have had a dearth of governmental leaders who cared how the place smells. Now and then some politicians have mentioned river pollution, but they have always done it just before they went out of office. A couple of governors spoke of the river and immediately retired from public life. The custom of mentioning the river has thus subsided somewhat, and our present gubernatorial incumbent appears not to know about the river. However, a few years back the industrialists evidently agreed the thing was pretty bad, and they made a gesture of appeasing the nose-holding voters.

This was an interesting thing to watch. After they had decided to let themselves be sued, I gather they carefully screened the state's justices. In this way they were able to confine the entire case to expensive argument over the basic question—Does the river really stink?

The courthouse is close by the river, and they had to keep the windows closed and an Air-wick going during the argument, but they were able to establish beyond a reasonable doubt that the river didn't stink at all. It presumably occurred to somebody that while this was an honest legal opinion, it might be hooted at in the great outdoors where a large and generous festoon of stench was evident on other than courtroom terms. Maine law was certainly in a quandary, but our justices and attorneys were equal to it. The decision was cloaked in the most profound legalistic verbiage, but in translation it ran about like this: The river does not stink, but we will try to make it smell better.

The industrialists were thus spared an order to go ahead and do something and were saved some expense. The legal fraternity was overjoyed at such an astute canter, and shortly the judge was cited by a colleague for having, "one of the keenest legal minds in Maine."

After the smell of the trial wore off, we could smell the river again, and it was just as bad. My keen nose carries no weight in court, however. The program called for settling reservoirs in which pulp mills would collect their brine, but they tell me one of the reservoirs was built with a hole in it so it could leak out in the river if it cared to. This may not be so, but I am willing to believe it if you insist. Then they got a Bates College professor who was to take a boat at stated intervals and dump nitrate in the river to counteract the brine which the mills weren't supposed to be dumping in any more. An industrial chemist with Dupont told me he didn't know of any reason why this should work, but perhaps it might. The professor has been doing it right along, and now and then he issues statements to the newspapers in which his experiment is hailed as a howling

53

success. This seems to bear out the judgment of the court, although many people are unconvinced.

There may be no flaw in the indenture, but we still have no fish in the river, paint continues to turn yellow, and we can still smell the thing three miles away. The lovely Androscoggin River is a reeking mess of filth and debris. Actually, there is no need of it. The laws of Maine as enacted long ago by pioneer lawmakers are still perfectly good laws because they have never been used. Our state government is full of elective and appointive officials who have full power to remedy the causes of our Androscoggin pollution. The same judge who officiated so gallantly over the definitions of stink could have just as readily produced a helpful answer. Indeed, the inter-state nature of the Androscoggin can be considered—which gives it a federal status.

But here we are living in a stench that, officially, doesn't exist. Fish, schooling 100 miles off in the ocean, can tell the Androscoggin when they come to it, and they turn aside. I don't blame them. If they were human beings, they'd probably come up anyway—attracted by the weekly payrolls, perhaps.

Well, I think use has spoiled a lot of things for us. Like the river. There's no need of it. The Androscoggin, today, could run clear and clean all the way to the sea. We don't have to let it stink, theoretically. We can rise up as citizens and demand our rights.

I wonder why we don't?

☙ ☙ ☙

*A couple of fallacies
completely exploded.*

WITH RECKLESS ABANDON I shall now dispose of two subjects at once: Candlemas Day and New Year's.

It appears we have two kinds of hand scythes. One was invented by some forward-looking farmer for cutting hay and grain, and much can be said about it—some of it with deep feeling and a voice that will carry for miles. The other kind was invented by cartoonists and appears in the newspapers every January First in the hands of that vigilant harvester, Father Time. This cartoonists' scythe has a curious design, and as a proficient hand mower I have never figured it out. If a cartoonist tried to mow with it he would make one swing and cut both legs off at the hips and would be all through for the day. If Father Time depended on it for his relentless duties, we would all be laughing joyfully in a kind of untouchable immortality.

I suppose the particular offset of a scythe sneath is elusive, and isn't studied much in art schools.

There aren't many people, in fact, who can pro-
nounce it—I gather that sneath, snath, sneth, snak,
and snat are all acceptable, and down beyond the
Penobscot they will give it an unblushing snarth.
So artists may be excused if they err on their first
attempt at rural verisimilitude. On the second
attempt, however, they ought to find out, and
there is no need of a perpetual, perennial error.
My own kind of a scythe was invented for cutting
grass and in the hands of a capable person it does
a first-rate job and needs no apologies. I dwell
on the subject because the scythe seems to be
passing out of our life except for the misdrawn
examples on New Year's Day.

Not long ago anybody around a farm could
mow with a scythe, and did. Grandfather has told
me how he and his brothers started out in the
dawn and mowed steadily until the climbing sun
had dried up the dew and they quit until dew fell
again in the afternoon. Grass mows best when it's
wet. Each brother would be a few paces ahead
of the next, and a good master of the works would
contrive to have a seasoned veteran with mature
intentions on the end. The steady rhythm of his
mowing was a constant rear-action threat to the
next son up ahead. The next son up ahead mowed
very well indeed, and communicated his enthusiasm on up the line. Everybody mowed himself
out of harm's way, and the hay wasn't long in
coming down.

One fine morning Grandfather showed me how to mow. He lectured and demonstrated together, and it was a short lesson: "Keep the point down, keep the heel down, stand up straight, don't try to cut too much, come 'way around, and then go away back, see?" The grass swished out to the left and lay in an ordered heap. The swath was wide and smooth, no dip in the center—every stubble was the same length. I tried it, but I kept the heel up, the point up, I stooped as if weeding carrots, tried to cut too much—and hit a rock.

This returned us to the grindstone where I lifted myself off the ground with each revolution of the handle, and Grandfather combined sharpening instructions with a lively story of how he shot a marsh hen during the second battle of Bull Run and made a very fine stew that evening. The boys were hungry, and it went very well with his company. Each edge of a scythe must be ground to the proper bevel, and the aim is to get a "wire edge" the whole length of the blade. That takes great skill on the grindstone, and much labor on the handle. Afterwards, the wire edge is cuffed off with a whetstone or a pine stick, and you are ready to go to mowing again.

In time I got onto it, and mowing is certainly one of those jobs where knowing how pays off. The sturdiest muscles can wilt to custards when a man bulls at it, but a little fellow who knows how can mow all day and still go to a dance at

57

night. Of course, even the little fellow has to stop and sit down now and then, and a jug of something to drink every time you go by a certain spot is a good idea.

In these times a machine does all the straight work and leaves only the trimmings to a scythe. One man can putter around after a tractor mower and not have enough hand mowing to keep him busy. But most farms around here do have some swales—swampy, wet runs where a tractor would bog down. The hay in the swales isn't worth much, it puts a cow to the trouble of ignoring it. But it makes bedding, or mulch, and you have to cut the swales for looks or to keep bushes from coming in. So the man with the scythe puts on some rubber boots and strikes into the swalegrass. Rubber boots are not productive of extreme agility, and if you watch such a mower he will pause now and then to pant.

Swalegrass doesn't dry out so readily as meadow hay, and as the sun climbs higher in the sky it is harder to find an excuse to stop. Long after the meadow mowers would be through for the morning, swalegrass is still cutting nicely. It is rank, heavy stuff, and you might think it would cut hard. It doesn't. Except for the exercise of motion you could go on and on. But who wants to go on and on? A prudent farmer will find an apple tree to hang his scythe in, or find he needs a touching up on the grindstone. After touching up, all manner

58

of other things to do present themselves. Swale-grass isn't worth too much fuss.

One of the nicest things about hand mowing, for the athlete who selects it to improve the condition of his anatomy, is the way it brings out parts of you that had thus far been ignored. You find places on you that you didn't know you had. It exercises your entire being in all directions. The only thing exactly like hand mowing, in this respect, is falling in a threshing machine—except that a man who falls in a threshing machine doesn't have to get up tomorrow and do it again.

Mowing, like many other manual tasks involving great skill, appears to be easy. This part of it affords the mower some fun now and then. Once or twice, maybe, a season a mower will be mowing away, swinging along gently with the rhythm of his work, when some victim shows up. The victim watches for a moment, and never having seen anybody mowing before the victim is delighted with what he has found. After a bit he says, "Let me try it." A good mower then hands over the scythe and goes to the stone wall to sit down and enjoy himself. The victim then does many wonderful things, most of which are beyond the ability of the human anatomy. He does not, however, cut much grass. After a bit he is willing to hand the scythe back to the farmer, who has no expression whatever on his sun-tanned face. The farmer will make two or three quick passes to smooth up the

59

wreckage done by the victim, and then catching his rhythm he will swing off down the swale making it look as if mowing is the easiest thing in the world.

My suggestion is merely that newspaper cartoonists be sent up here so they can get acquainted with scythes. I can give them a couple of lessons, and Father Time will henceforth have a useful scythe that he can swing in his macabre way and mow down whatever he wants to without hacking off his whiskers instead.

As to woodchucks, there may be places where one comes out on February second to gaze about and indicate the weather, but in this latitude the legend of a Candlemas groundhog is as misshapen as Father Time's scythe handle. The woodchuck hibernates, and his appearance in the spring coincides with the sprouting of the green peas—which is much later than February second. A woodchuck who comes out before the peas are ready to eat is crazy. But every Candlemas our newspapers cover the woodchuck situation in detail, and a novice reporter who couldn't find a story in the complete works of O. Henry always seems to be able to step out on February second and find a groundhog to interview. The interview is given prominence in the evening editions, and nicely uses up space that might otherwise be devoted to information which would justify the subscriber's financial support.

The whole thing is absurd. No real farmer in this vicinity is fooled. The woodchuck, so vividly pictured in the evening paper, is still asleep. Along in May he will rouse, flex his muscles and give his appetite setting up exercises, and then he will awaken his family and come out to start at one end of the peas and clean out the whole row.

The farmer will contrive to be there about that time, and he will aim a large, old-fashioned, single-barrel 12-gauge shotgun at said woodchuck and pull the trigger with a reverberating finality. The untimely demise of the newspaper's perennial favorite will have no news stature whatever. Farmers' love for br'er Chuck is the lowest form of nonexistence.

It's kind of curious, too. People speak good words for hawks and owls, snakes and foxes, and even the skunk gets a pat on the back for his useful habits. But a woodchuck seems to have no redeeming features. Out on the farm a dog isn't worth his keep if he can't account for chucks every season. And the way a dog goes into a frenzy when he corners a woodchuck suggests a hatred even pussycats can't excite. Big farm collies who can do everything but tat will become raving maniacs when they corner a chuck in a stone wall, and they'll bark themselves inside out until somebody comes running to move a rock.

And to show you how nasty and mean a woodchuck is, it's surprising how often one of them turns out to be a skunk or a porcupine, which is a dirty trick on any dog, and should not be tolerated by respectable citizens. A dog who loyally defends his master's acres by waging relentless war on all woodchucks deserves some protection on this score. People who have a dog who, chasing a woodchuck, suddenly discovers the woodchuck is a skunk, can see at once how sad this makes the dog. It affects his morale, and leads him to be forever distrustful. During his long exile he reflects and ruminates on his sad lot, and despondency sets in. But that is a woodchuck for you, and shows how things are.

A woodchuck who turns out to be a porcupine isn't quite such a stinker, to quote Oliver Wendell Holmes, but he does have a similar unhappy effect on the dog. The other day our dog cornered a woodchuck in the stone wall and we heard him give off a few peals of delight, after which he yiped once and then ran across the seventeen-acre field with his tail completely out of sight. At suppertime he came back to the house, but crawled under the stove and showed slight interest in the family conversations. Somebody discovered he had white things on his face, so we got the pliers from the barn and set to work.

Operating on a dog who has been fouled up by a porcupine, even if he thought it was a woodchuck, is not too hard a job. While the quills seem to cause excruciating inconvenience in the flesh, the dog appears to be relieved the instant they are removed. Some dogs, more knowing than others, will lay their pincushion noses on your knee and let you pull. Some fight it a little and you have to be persuasive. Some snap and you have to wedge a stovewood stick between their teeth. An old hound we had, placid beyond belief, would go stark, raving mad when he got some quills, and we always had to wrap him in a blanket, put a stick in his mouth, and hold him by brute strength.

Porcupine quills are barbed and work into flesh. If they aren't removed they will continue to penetrate, and if they hit some vital that's the end. They may work themselves out in time by their own action. But somebody discovered once that if you take a pair of manicure scissors and snip off the end of the quill, it will deflate and lose its ability to penetrate. In a day or so it will drop out, or can be pulled out by the fingers at the time. But from the standpoint of an operating surgeon, it's often much easier to be forthright and just yank the quills out with pliers. A whining, twisting, reluctant dog, wrapped in a blanket, makes it just as hard to snip quills as to pull them. So you pull. After you get the last one out the dog jumps up all friendly, has himself a long drink of water, and like as not will go out the next day and tackle another woodchuck with quills. Some dogs learn, some don't.

At the time our dog went through this unhappy experience, he kept up a continued run of comment, telling me a lot about woodchucks that I will not repeat. I thought at the time that this was an interview the newspaper boys might well use to convey the truth of their Candlemas proposition. The dog said that was just like a woodchuck, to turn out to be a porcupine, and he was going to say a lot more when a woman called up from over in the next town and wanted to know what in heaven's name we were doing to our dog. Her reaction to our reply was informative.

We told her the dog got a porcupine. Instead of commiserating with the dog, she said, "Damned woodchucks!" That's about the size of it.

So even if a woodchuck came out on February second, and even if he did prognosticate the weather, there isn't a farmer around here who would believe the bugger, and that's that.

I hope we hear no more about this foolishness of Candlemas forecasts, and that Father Time henceforth has a scythe he can work with.

*Hell isn't any
    too hot.*

THEOLOGIANS DO PRETTY WELL WITH
their tales of an everlasting bonfire, but I'd like
to have one. I'd boil maple syrup on it. I've been
feeding the vernal holocaust over which we reduce
our maple sap to sugar, and it takes quite a bit
of feeding. Pyro-perpetual torment may frighten
some people.

It takes about a cord of wood to make 15 gallons of maple syrup—some figure a little more,
some less. Anyone who makes 300 gallons, a good
season's quantity, therefore burns something like
20 cords of wood. The season, roughly, is some
portion of March—which means that the intensity
of the fire is a good imitation of perdition. It

65

makes a man an authority on heat, and after a long, hard winter it's kind of pleasant to sit there basking and stoking. While basking and stoking I got to thinking about Henry Ford.

One year we made some money on turnips and we went off to see some expensive things. We got to Henry Ford's Greenfield Village and got acquainted with perpetual fires. Mr. Ford seemed to have a passion for them, and the hired guides who take turnip growers about the place make the most of the arrangement.

In one place there's a little donkey engine, something Thomas A. Edison had, and as a memorial to the Wizard of Menlo Park they have kindled a perpetual fire in the boiler. I'm no hand to go sight-seeing—I'm always anxious about things back home and don't pay too much attention. But being an authority on heat, the fire interested me and I stepped ahead in the crowd and inquired. I asked the guide if the fire ever went out accidentally when the janitor overslept, or the maintenance superintendent had gone off to Ypsilante on a jag. The guide ignored me and began on another paragraph of his prepared speech. I asked him if they went and told Mr. Ford whenever that happened. I never got quite so much ignore in any other place.

I was sorry that the practical aspects of this matter were so unimportant to other people, and so unimportant to the guide. Mr. Ford, in his day, was a most practical man, and in his youth before he became wealthy and detached he must have gone around asking just such questions as mine. He must have noticed, in his formative days, that a man who cuts wood is often sparing in the burning of it. If I had to cut wood for a perpetual fire, I think I would stint occasionally on hot nights when nobody was around.

This Greenfield Village is a fine thing, but it's no place for a New Englander. All the things we grew up with and have around us from day to day are embalmed and treasured up at Greenfield Village as if they had gone from the face of the earth. People from Baltimore and Lansing and St. Louis and Denver come there and see these museum pieces and gasp at the sheer ingenuity of them. The guide pointed at an ox-sling Mr. Ford has saved for posterity in a prominent place, and everybody in the crowd thought it was a very clever thing. It is, most everybody around home has one, and I don't know of any other way to get shoes on a steer. I hadn't thought of it before, but I could see it was ingenious. The guide didn't know how it worked, however, and where he had been so terse about the fire I hesitated to intrude any information. Some of the people from Denver asked how it worked, but the guide and I did not tell them.

It was the same with the covered bridge. Mr.

67

Ford engaged an excavator at great expense to manufacture a meandering river, and had thrown a covered bridge across it at one point to give the guides something else to show. The crowd thought it was wonderful. One woman, possibly seeking information, asked what the bridge was for. Thinking back on the occasion, I find it is hard to attach inflections to these conversations. I know the woman asked what the bridge was for, but I can't recall if her tone was academic, or more inclined to social whimsy. The guide was able to continue his narrative without losing the course of his exposition, and the lady looked disappointed. She had asked the question in a clear, distinct voice, and as a kind of museum quiet hung over the region, mellowed slightly by the distant tinkle of some Stephen Foster melody where that gentleman was being memorialized by a perpetual song, there was no reason why the guide shouldn't have heard her. He did not, however, and I felt I ought to help.

I said, "It's to cross the river on."

The lady looked at me, the way any true citizen of the golden west will transfix anybody from the effete and retrogressive east, and indicated that while she didn't believe me, she felt I was bold in expecting her to. The rest of the crowd gasped at my rashness, so to support my contention I added, "We got lots of them back home." I was going to tell them about the signs up under the

68

eaves—old circus posters, bills for Sweet Caporal cigarettes, and the weathered notices at each end saying that if you don't walk your horse they'll fine you $1. If the atmosphere had been congenial, I could have told them a lot about covered bridges —things in general like how the planks rumbled under a load of hay, or things in particular like the time Hezzy Potts tried to go through the bridge over Sims's brook with a twenty-five-foot timber on his hayrack crosswise. It set the bridge over a good deal. But I let the subject drop, and the people moved away from me then. The guide gave me a look and went on with his address.

I suppose those people think to this day that Henry Ford invented the covered bridge just as he did the planetary transmission. Of course, Mr. Ford's bridge, properly endowed, will be in Green-field Village long after our last covered bridge has been demolished by unsentimental state highway crews, and that will be good. I was talking to the road superintendent of the St. Johnsbury and Lake Champlain Railroad once about the covered bridges on his line, and I wondered if the coal-burning locomotives weren't a hazard when they churned through the structures. I said, "I should think the bridges would catch fire."

He said, "They do." There is a great deal of Vermont in that colloquy, but very little of Henry Ford. Mr. Ford's museum piece will remain intact, safe for future generations, interesting and unique

—even if nobody knows what it's for. I felt about the same over his New England Town Hall. It is a lovely thing, charming in its nicely curried fidelity to Yankee tradition. But a small, neatly lettered sign on the front says, "It has no historical significance." That's like setting up a statue of Thomas B. Reed and saying, "He never amounted to much." As the incidence of pure democracy falters and fails (even, alas, in New England) it might be well to regard the remotest facsimile as a useful reminder—even if the New England Meeting House finally dwindles to a single example in far-off Michigan.

But all the time this was going on, we kept running into perpetual fires. Mr. Ford's passion for perpetual fires began to make me worry about him. As I recollect, there were perpetual fires for Edison, Herbert Hoover, Stephen Foster, Tommy Manville, Eric the Red, Homer Rhodeheaver, and Abraham Lincoln. I think there was one for McGuffey's Eclectic Readers, but I'm not sure about the Wright Brothers. I couldn't remember everything.

The fire for Lincoln was quite a good one, but the ashes needed cleaning out. I would like to have the ashes to put on my grapevine. The fireplace was in a room full of Lincoln relics, and it was very hot there. This was in July, and it would have been hot there anyway. I gathered that keeping the Lincoln fire in perpetuity had been worked up into an effective little drama, intended to impress the tourist. The crowd assembled in the little room and the guide was about mid-point of his remarks when he called attention to the man about to place fuel on the perpetual fire for the Great Emancipator. The man had not yet appeared, but upon this cue he stepped briskly in the door with a Barrymore approach, a couple of two-foot sticks in his arm. I couldn't make out what kind of wood it was, but it wasn't beech or maple. We like beech and maple at home. This man shouldered his way through the crowd and laid his sticks on the Lincoln Fire. The guide turned his head aside discreetly so we could not see him brush off the salt tears that were streaming down his face as he still mourned our late president. He was able to get a grip on himself presently, and continued his narration about the courtroom in which Lincoln tried his first case. The bearer of wood tip-toed out of the room, looking less like the eulogizer of the immortal and more like a man who gets a good day's pay for a snap. Mr. Ford, unlike me, could afford to hire a man to keep his fires going.

But he does keep the fires going. They are continuous, interminable, inextinguishable blazes —each producing a terrific heat which passes up the chimney or dissipates itself unused in the vicinity. The gesture wasn't lost on me—I appreciate the solemn veneration Mr. Ford felt for those he honored. That was his way of showing respect, and with his funds he must be accorded some freedom of choice.

But it's a shame to waste all that heat.

What I'm coming at is this: I'd like to have them move one of the perpetual fires to Maine. The endowment to run it could be spent here just as well as in Michigan, and every spring I could make maple syrup on it.

❀ ❀ ❀

Poor old biddy
needs sympathy.

WHENEVER THERE'S NOTHING ELSE to do I sit around and think about the poor hen. What's happened to her is a shame, and I see some government expert says he hasn't been able to find the perfect hen. He is going to keep trying, but it looks doubtful. When you get a government expert to admit he's stumped, it's worth noticing, so that's something, but I went out and asked one of my hens what she thought of this announcement.

She said it was all right with her. She said she hadn't found the perfect government expert, either, and everything was in balance. Personally, I think my hen is perfect, and no government expert has ever come to survey her. She doesn't

72

look like much, and in places her foliage has deciduated and left her looking like a boiled frankfurt, but with laudable concentration on more important things she has gone along as if we didn't notice. My hen said things have come to a pretty pass in general, and at times she got sick and tired of trying to amount to anything.

She said, "There was a time people knew hens, and there was some point in the business, but today all they want is an egg-plant, a precision tool, something to set up a bookkeeping system about. You used to look at a hen and tell what she was—a Blue Andalusian, a Buff Orpington, a Dominique. But today they holler about sex-linking and R.O.P., and a hen that has any resemblance to a good, old-fashioned barnyard lady is held up to ridicule.

"You take me, now. I look like hell in these abbreviated culottes, but in another three weeks I'll have my feathers in, and I'll look pretty good. I'll look like a hen. Why, my grandmother got washed in a tub of soap and water once, with bluing, and went to a hen show and won her owner a twenty-dollar hat that he still wears, and Grammie never laid more than twelve or fifteen eggs a year in her life. If Grammie hadn't anything else, she had class. But I was reading a government bulletin the other day, and the man said you could usually tell a good bird by the unkempt plumage. Well, you can tell an expert when he says bird for hen, but it always seemed to me feathers kind of made the hen, and in the old days you won damned few hats unless you had some."

My hen has picked up a few words here and there. I have always tried to keep loud, coarse talk from the farm animals, but now and then some hired hand forgets himself.

My hen continued, "What these government experts want is something else again. They want a hen as bare as an inner tube, all ready for the market without plucking. They want something that will burst from the egg and grow up to seven pounds in a week. Something that will make a market return with a minimum of capital investment. What they ought to do is forget all about hens, let hens alone, and start from scratch along a new and different line. This business of looking upon us hens as plain open-and-shut collateral is, frankly, kind of insulting. The perfect hen they're looking for isn't a hen at all—they want something like a magician's hat. A machine of some kind with no bones in it, no feathers—something like a squash that turns out eggs all squared up for the case. While I have my strength I'm going to be a hen, and nothing else but a hen, and along with the eggs I manage to turn out you're going to have to put up with a lot of plain henneryness."

I told my hen that I sometimes mentioned her in my literary capacity, and it was always a favorable delineation. I told her I was satisfied in every way. I said I was discerning, and I knew that charm and personality were computable qualities, fully as much as weight and number of eggs. I said I had thought it all over, having heard both sides of the question, and that I didn't want a perfect hen. I said I just wanted an old-fashioned one so I could look out the kitchen window and see her tail feathers rumpled in a southerly wind, and know it was going to rain.

She thanked me at that, and said for her part the whole thing was reciprocal, and if I'd do my part she felt quite sure I would find out that she'd do hers.

I have always claimed that the hen is man's greatest feathered friend, and I have resisted the Audubon Society because of their limited horizon. They want me to love the bluebird, and immediately I found that the first bluebird, harbinger of spring, was a cock-eyed liar. He came and sang over my lintel and told me to rejoice, that warm weather was at hand, the awakening world was about to rise and shine and all creation was in the throes of jubilation and delight. Then he went away and we froze up. That year we had practically no summer at all—the snowbank by the barn never quite receded entire, but winter coming added more before winter going had finished thawing. I like the birds, but I don't think the hen is properly treated by the bird lovers. They could do more than they have for her.

The old-time hen is, of course, a dead duck. A gone goose. Dame Partlett, the Little Red Hen, Chicken-Little and Henny-Penny have no counterpart in this age. People today can't tell a Brahma rooster from a litter of beagles, and they could find beagles a good deal sooner than they could find a Brahma rooster. Today the hen is an inoculated nonentity in a flock of 50,000 "birds" working in precise unison in one of these great poultry factories where the lights burn all night. The romance is gone. It is sad.

In a farm magazine a while ago they had a story on the poultry industry's great publicity program, put on at great expense to teach children in the schools something about the hen and the egg. The New England Poultry and Egg Institute had gone to 922 school assemblies and had shown its movies and given its little talks to 280,000 pupils. They felt they were making great headway.

And yet, I think the great need for ovoid education in our schools is occasioned, largely, by the fact that Henny-Penny is now so seldom. My youngster, with the egg on his necktie, is not unaware of the great boon known as the hen. He has a flock of eight lovely Henny-Pennies, with a large rooster in charge, and every morning before school he has to go out and water them, feed them, and lay out the day's work. Every night after school he has to go out and collect his eggs. In this way he has learned many things the poultry industry spends money to inculcate in others.

The hen does not fly south in the winter like swallows, and does not hibernate under a rock like frogs. She doesn't sing good, but she does it loud and shows enthusiasm. She is one of the oldest advocates of publicity, and has long been a consistent user of advertising space. The happy boy who learns his poultry lore firsthand can sit at his kitchen table, eating a new-laid egg on the half shell, and the hen can still be heard through the window advertising the event in all directions. Then when the weather warms the hen humps up and gets broody, and in three weeks will hatch me some baby chicks, bringing them out from under a woodpile with great industry. Most baby birds look disreputable and moth-eaten—but a tiny fuzz of down sticking out from under a red-hot Rhode Island Red is a first-rate bird for my money, and Audubon can lump it. They lay eggs on a descending market, and I still spend $6 a bag for their grain. I wouldn't do that for any Bob-o-link that ever lived.

All this, of course, and a rooster, too. My rooster is quite gentlemanly, and has a crow that will part your hair. His labors are not arduous, and I let him lay out his own schedule. But part of his career is to be prominent in the life about the old homestead, and I wouldn't want him shut away in the teeming cells of a modern egg factory.

Nobody knows what goes on in those sweatshops except the specialists in the business, and they have to employ public relations men to translate the technical matter into school-age paraphrases. What they know has to be presented with activated charts, play-time drolleries and vivid motion pictures. By running the film backward they can make the chicken go back in the egg, and this salubriates the schoolboy attitude so he is alert and attentive. The poultry industry has forgotten that eight hens and a rooster can say everything their high-priced publicists can say, and do it much better.

I think every growing child should have eight hens and a rooster to instruct him, and people will now remind me that you can't very well keep hens in an apartment or under suburban zoning laws. I can only say that I know of no statute requiring people to live in apartments or in the vicinity of zoning restrictions. There are millions of acres of wild land yet undeveloped in our outlying sections, upon any of which Henny-Penny can survive if given reasonable attention. Children who care for them might not enjoy the blessings of crowded urban schools, but they would not have to sit through an assembly while some publicity man demonstrates that basic knowledge is now merely a business instrument. The general idea of the poultrymen is to get people to eat eggs.

I quote from that article: "Many nutritionists and educators have told the writer that an understanding of the operations of the farmer as he feeds the soil, plants and animals to produce good food is one of the best introductions to the teaching of practical, everyday, personal nutrition." This understanding gears the pupil for the tense life of office and factory, etc., and so on. It also furthers the established program of modern agronomy, in which the hen must also be geared to the tense life of the scientific dormitory with 2,800 windows.

The business of burning lights all night in modern poultry palaces has the effect of neutralizing the solar system. Our rooster brings the sun up every morning. He really does. One morning he arose a little early, it was May and his ambitions were springlike, and he crowed with his usual vigor, and the sun came up a half-hour early. He was ashamed of himself, and some of the neighbors complained. But the incident proved how important a rooster can be in the family plan.

The size of the domestic flock is very important. I think eight is about right. That gives you all the eggs you want, and doesn't strain your financial structure. When larger flocks are maintained, eggs must be sold at a loss and you are immediately in trouble with your internal revenue office. The big poultrymen of modern times live on deductions and can spend their summers abroad by showing an excess of cost over net, but a little fellow can't do that. Sometime you want to try explaining to an income tax man that you have charged off part of your motor vehicle expense to a superannuated rooster merely because he has a nice crow and you regard him as a symbol of lost horizons. When you have 10,000 roosters you can do that. You can also charge off something for support of a publicity man who goes to schools and shows movies.

I can remember when the great change came over poultry, and the hen changed from a personality to a business index. In my youth the word "utility" had not been heard. There was a book called the American Standard of Perfection, which pictured all the established breeds of hens and set up qualifications. Every year we held a poultry show and it was a good deal more fun than a horse trot. Everybody had his favorite breed, and knew a hen from a duck without needing a government bulletin to explain the essential varietal differences, as the poet puts it. The man who had Black Minorcas was proud of his strain, and the man who had Silver Spangled Hamburgs was equally so. We had American Dominiques—the little old speckled hen that stood underfoot in all pioneer literature. Men with White Orpingtons really did wash them with bluing, and also shined toenails and lacquered beaks. Some people

80

looked and saw hens, but we saw a high degree of art and showmanship.

A big event during the three-day poultry show was the supper and annual meeting. After the cigars were passed, and I always took one in spite of my youth so I could take it home for Father, the officers would be elected for the next year, and we would have a speaker. One year the speaker was a man from the University of Maine and he used a new and strange word. He said, "Utility." This was a prophetic speech, and in a few short years the utility program put our fine old poultry show on the blink and we went out of business. We owned hundreds of exhibition coops and pine tables to set them on, but the poultry show was a goner.

In the philosophy of utility, there is no such thing as a disqualification. A Dominique can have a single comb, feathers on her leg, and red feathers. If she can lay an egg with some rapidity and continuity, she is a hen. Birds that made a monkey of the Standard of Perfection would hump up when the judge came by and lay an egg, and win a blue ribbon. Art was no longer important. The pure strains of distinct breeds went out of style in the newer search for utility poultry—high production, heavy salvage value, application to duty. These were the things that paid off. The State Department of Agriculture, which had always sent a stipend to encourage fancy poultry, now paid off only to those shows that promoted utility.

The cross-bred hen became a passion. I've always worried a little over what happens with the cross-breeders in all branches of farming when they no longer have any pure strains to cross. When all the world is a mongrel, who will be basic? But the old breeds have gone. There probably isn't a pure Dominique hen in existence today, but once they were common, and they were used to produce all other American breeds by lending their better qualities to a mixture. Some day somebody might like to start all over again, but the Dominique will not be there to help.

But that is the consequence of affairs. When "keeping a few hens" became known as "poultry management," the thing was done. If a Silver Spangled Hamburg looked like a hoot owl with one eye gone, but could lay eggs, she would win a prize as a Silver Spangled Hamburg, and one year when a flock of Barred Plymouth Rocks took all the prizes for Dominiques, just because they weighed more on the hoof, we could see that the future was dim. My father had a rooster that he offered to sell for fifty dollars, a most reasonable price, but there were no takers so we ate him for Sunday dinner. Father still brags about the expensive meal we had. This rooster was the grandson of the very male and female Dominiques pictured in the American Standard of Perfection. If you wanted a Dominique, he was the very best in the world. He was grand champion at the Madison Square Garden Poultry Show, and had been to the World Poultry Congress at Melbourne, Australia. He had blue ribbons enough so Mother made a quilt from them. He was also tougher than gum overshoes when we ate him.

The sun's coming up has nothing to do with Utility.

But Utility has won, and the poultry barracks that dot our landscape show how things are now. Striving ever onward and upward, the specialists are still seeking that nebulous goal—the perfect hen. At times they think maybe they have her, but she fails them. Perhaps her fertility is .056% short. Maybe she needs one extra pound of grain to hit the market, or perhaps she needs four days too many to start laying. Her ability to foretell a storm by standing at the sinkspout, backed into the wind, is of no consequence. The era has gone. Times have changed. The cackle of the biddy and the clarion call of her jubilant mate can no longer deliver proper public relations, dollar for dollar. The industry goes into the schools and shows movies.

I didn't want to tell my hen as much, but I think she's about perfect. She goes broody when she pleases, and sometimes sits for days on an old jelly tumbler. When she starts to lay, super-sensory perceptions have already told her the egg market is in a slump. She wots not of fish-liver oil and calcium concentrates, but still digs angleworms under my rhubarb. For amusement she often dusts herself in the petunias. She likes me, and pecks the eyelets on my boots. I like her, and make a little acceptance speech when I gather the fruits of her success.

I think when there is nothing else going on, again, I shall think about the hen some more.

❀ ❀ ❀

Scarcely anybody
gets killed.

NOW OUR QUIET OLD ACRES COME to life and the noise of the shootgun is heard in the land. It is hunting season in Maine. The happy housewife, singing *I'll Be Coming, Sister Mary* through a clothespin as she takes in the Monday wash, finds her damask tablecloth punched full of No. 6 holes, and the prudent husbandman wears red hat and shirt when he steps out to the privy.

It is a noisy time, the tumultuous cannonade mingled with the shrieks of the wounded and the groans of the dying, and all Maine citizens conduct themselves beyond the call of duty. In ordinary years we will bag more deer than we do hunters, and some years when the conditions are favorable hardly anybody gets killed.

Two years ago I was sitting where I am now, in a front window that gives onto the mailbox and highway, and my every attention was engrossed on a reply to a gentleman who had written to me about a sum of money. I had spelt "lousy" with a "w," and was erasing my error when the First Battle of the Marne took place directly outside my window. The room is only eight feet square, but I trotted around it a good deal with one foot shoved in the waste basket, and then I looked out to see what had occasioned this unrest on my part. A large, florid gentleman with St. Vitus's dance was leaning one elbow on my window sill and shooting with amazing rapidity into the general direction of north. Whatever he was shooting at was beyond the immediate panorama, and I had to move to look. As I did so, a spike-horn buck deer decided he had endured enough of life's misfortunes, and he gave up the ghost and died at the foot of an apple tree which we have always considered to be on the front lawn. I assumed that in spite of his obvious nervous condition the gentleman over whose shoulder I was peering had connected in some strange way and had, as the saying goes, "got his deer."

The gentleman continued to shoot off and on while I opened the window, and then I spoke to him softly and said, "You can stop shooting now, he's dead."

The gentleman then turned two glassy eyes upon me and said, with some degree of accuracy, "I got him! I got him!"

This appeared to be so, and I saw no reason to dispute it, so I said, "Put your gun on safety, you're all done for this year."

At this the gentleman fired two or three more times, lopping a large limb off the apple tree, and I reached out and pushed the safety catch on his firearm. Then when he pulled the trigger nothing happened. This surprised him, and brought some light back into his eyes and caused him to hand me the gun, which I took inside the house and unloaded.

One thing about the chase that I have found amusing is the question of what you do now. The fun-loving sportsman who dons his gay garb, picks up his accouterments, and strikes out to slay the white-tailed deer is in pretty good shape until he shoots something. Immediately the frolicsome deer, who can bound across country like sin, is no longer a sporty quarry, but suddenly becomes a couple of cwt. of meat. A slaughter house is equipped to handle same, and in the proper place a venison carcass presents no great problem. But the hunter, hiding behind his Fish & Game Club badge, is no longer a hunter, he's a wholesale owner of fresh meat and he has to take care of it.

Somebody who has journeyed five miles into the uncharted fastnesses to shoot a 300-pound buck is immediately very sorry that he was so ambitious. The deer that you chased out has to be carried back.

The gentleman leaning against my house told me he had never shot a deer before. I said, "Well, you have now," and I thought it was quite a witty remark. We unsheathed a knife and dressed out the deer, but the gentleman to whom the meat belonged didn't know how to do it, and he kept walking back and forth saying, "I got him, I got him." I noticed he was still holding his hands out, thinking he still held the rifle, and every little while his right index finger would twitch.

I hadn't intended to mention this, but I fell to thinking very few people have had the pleasure of just such an experience in quite such close surroundings. I am not of a shooting turn of mind myself, and the deer in my dooryard usually come and go as they please. We have to shoo them once in a while to get out to the henhouse, but they come right back. I resented this man's interrupting me in the middle of a sentence, but he had a license and the deer belong to the people of the state.

A neighbor woman who saw a deer out her kitchen window ran to the gunrack and got a gun and shot the deer. It cost eighteen dollars to put the glass back, but she got him, and he weighed

235 pounds. Her husband was out hunting at the time, but he didn't get anything.

As a detached witness of this annual scene, I can report that the hunting season in Maine is less bloody than the antishoot faction makes out. It does give the undertakers a welcome flurry between the summer tourist season and early-winter pneumonia, but from the point of view of our dear woodland friends it is not too tough. I have an old bull partridge who lives up by the spring in my pasture, and every April when we are on the tag end of the maple syrup season he begins to drum and advertise that his hen is expecting. Our so-called partridge is actually a ruffed grouse, or—as the political naturalists in our Maine Development Commission continue to spell him—a *ruffled* grouse. Sometimes he is more ruffled than others, but you will find him in your Audubon book under the former name, and he is one of the finest birds we have. Unlike the imported pheasant, he stays where he belongs in the woods, and never bothers pay crops up in the fields. So every April I know that my partridge is about to multiply, and I sneak through the bushes and try to catch him drumming. He inflates his breast, or at least swells it out somehow, and then beats his wings against himself rhythmically —gaining speed as he goes. The first blows are staccato, but on the end his finale is a whirr. He almost lifts himself off the ground in flight, and seems to hang by his toes to the log he sits on. After drumming he sits quietly or parades a little, and at intervals day after day he drums until the eggs hatch. People who don't know about drumming always think it sounds like a gasoline motor of some sort in the distance.

Well, what I'm coming at is that the partridge is always there in the spring, and he is there off and on all summer when I go up to pick berries, and then one day the hunting season is on and my woods are full of red-shirted sportsmen who are trying to shoot my partridges. All day the guns resound. A stratum of lead lies on the ground, the Getchell Birches are riddled, and ever and anon the coroner comes and sits on somebody. Each morning the hunters come and whack the puckerbrush, and each evening they go home. But after the hunting season is over and I go up in my woods to catch a little firewood, I always find my partridges as before. They explode up from underfoot and scale away. And the next spring the old bull partridge is always drumming away in a uxorious trance, or an uxorious trance as the case may be.

It is the same with our deer. Somebody is always getting one by accident, but I notice that the deer I grow up with all summer are for the most part alive and well when it comes time to yard out in the cedars for winter. They sometimes look tired, but they are all right.

I've wondered if maybe my game isn't smarter than most. According to the official statements of our Fish & Game Commissioner, a lot of wildlife is done in every fall in Maine, but on the basis of my own domestic surveys there's little of it done in right here. I think my salubrious location and what Caesar would have termed the nature of the place contributes smartness to my wildlife. I can offer a case in point to support my opinion.

One night a knock came to our door and I opened it to find a band of 'coon hunters who wanted to know if our back woodlot abounded in said animal. I said we had a lot of them, that some days I kept stepping on them while I was working around. They asked if I cared to have them sport a little in that section, and I said yes, that if they'd wait until I got my boots on I'd go with them and watch. I said I'd been inside all day, papering a room, and a breath of air would do me good. So I checked to see that my last will and testament were handy and could be found should occasion require it, and we all went up on the beech ridge and down into the softwood growth.

They had a fine dog by the name of Duke, and he had a pedigree as long as the delinquent tax list in the town of Bowdoin. Duke had been imported from Ohio a short time before, and a great deal of interest was current over his skill. Duke was eager. They unsnapped him and away he went, bugling until the region resounded. The cry of a 'coon hound in the woods on a frosty night is a magnificent arrangement.

"What's he got?" somebody said.

Somebody else said, "Sounds as big as a cow!"

It struck me at the time that wondering what a 'coon dog would be chasing indicated doubt over the dog to begin with. I don't know much about Ohio 'coon dogs, but if I invested in one and paid the express on him, I would expect him to chase 'coons. This is only an opinion, and I may have the wrong slant.

Anyway, the bugling suddenly ceased, ta-ra, and back came Duke with his face stuck full of porcupine quills. We took him up to the house and spent the rest of the night pulling out quills. One of the sportsmen was a dentist, and he knew how to pull, so we let him pull. I understand they shipped Duke back to Ohio the next day, collect.

But you can't tell me my 'coons didn't rig up a scheme with that particular porcupine, and that while we were leading Duke home some forty or fifty intellectual 'coons weren't sitting around on pine limbs chuckling at a great rate. A dog that can't tell a porcupine from a 'coon is not so unusual as to be noteworthy, but one named Duke that has been shipped in from Ohio at great expense ought to know a little more than the average. That's the only time I ever went 'coon hunting.

My observation is that game keeps increasing every year. Hunters come in droves to shoot my foxes, but at night the foxes come and steal my ducks. They claim foxes eat pheasants, but every year we have more and more pheasants and more and more foxes, and it's harder and harder to raise up ducks. One reason is that people out hunting foxes occasionally shoot one of my ducks.

I like wildlife. I like to roam the farm and see the animals and birds around me. Every once in a while somebody asks me why I don't post my land and stop this cruel slaughter. Well, one reason I don't is because I think the animals like the hunting season. It quickens their reflexes, and I think they find the season exciting. They keep their heads down, and hunting seasons come and go, and it adds piquancy to an otherwise uneventful life.

We have a favorite deer who likes our upper orchard. She's been around for years, and brings up her young ones more or less in sight of the house. Sometimes we take summer visitors up along the wall and point her out. With her fawn, or sometimes twin fawns, she will be chewing on the orchard grass, and she'll lift her head and look at us and go back to eating. When the people go back to the cities they say, "Think of it! A deer right in the field back of the house!" I'd hate to have anything happen to this old girl.

Last year a fellow with an ammunition belt around his red jacket came, and he had a rifle that will shoot five miles. He went up in my orchard to seek out this doe. He found her, and took a shot at her. The bullet whistled over our house and hit Smith's barn. Well, this fellow shot at the deer all afternoon. She would dodge behind a tree and eat until he found her again, and then while he shot a few times she would dodge behind another tree. She gave him a great variety of shots, and no two alike. Now and then the hunter would have to wait for his gun barrel to cool off, and we would see him sitting under a tree eating one of our apples. Along about dusk he came down and got in his automobile and drove away.

For the most part, I think that is about the way our hunting season works out. There's a lot of noise, and now and then we hear a bullet slap into the clapboards, and once in a while we have to stop husking corn and go up in the woods and bring out a wounded hunter. Bringing out a wounded hunter wouldn't be so bad if you didn't have to listen to his companion explain how he looked like a deer. The best one I ever heard was about a young fellow up back who shot his own mother while she was paddling a canoe down the river. She came down the river and he up and shot her. He said he thought she was a partridge, and probably he did. When a fellow has a gun in his hand it's funny how many things look like a partridge. One time we were carrying a corpse out through a fence, and the fellow was explaining how his companion looked just like a deer. Jud

Maybury was on one of the feet, and Jud asked, "Buck or doe?"

The fellow didn't know Jud was joking, so he said he kind of thought he looked more like a doe.

Jud wagged his head all afternoon and spent the rest of the season down cellar back of the furnace reading the Waverley Novels. Jud was never much of a reader, but he had to occupy his time.

We always feel badly, of course, when some of our pet game gets knocked off, but the untimely demise of our sportsmen is not looked upon as a great loss. To illustrate the Maine attitude toward this, I shall cite an instance of a couple of seasons back. I would not want people to think we are callous about it. In every instance the guilty hunter is subjected to the severity of a court trial, although when he is a member of the governor's council or something like that a certain deference is always shown to his capacity. (I had not intended to use the word capacity in such way that it would constitute a hilarious joke, but I can't control the attitudes of my readers, and if you so take it, so be it.)

Well, in this case I speak of, the gentleman had whanged his wife at a distance of about fifteen feet right between the eyes with a large caliber rifle, and she was mortified. The gentleman immediately deposed and stated that he thought she was a deer, and to make his position more secure he added that while he knew his wife had been out hunting with him, he had come to the conclusion, only a moment before, that she had gone home. Therefore, not expecting his wife to be in the vicinity, when he saw her it was the most natural thing in the world to presume that she was a deer.

This case was reported in the newspapers at the time substantially as I now retell it, and is on record in our courts.

The judge in this case was, as you can see, forced to adjudicate a great deal. His decision was straightforward and to the point, and quite in keeping with the high quality of jurisprudence now being enjoyed in Maine. He said that a gentleman out hunting with his wife has the right to presume, at any time, that she has gone home, and that if a husband so presumes, the wife is guilty of contributory negligence if she remains in the vicinity. This decision was widely applauded, and I understand that upon releasing the respondent, the judge invited him to give a humorous talk at the next meeting of the Bar Association. So you can see that the situation in the Maine woods is under control at all times.

I would like to say in concluding this discussion that the state is not unmindful of certain civil obligations to its inhabitants, and that a Representative Bubar from the town of Blaine arose in legislature recently and proposed that hunting license fees be increased by seventy-five cents, so the state would have a fund to pay $5,000 to the widow of any hunter shot in the woods. Mr. Bubar (I am not sure if I pronounce that correctly) was deadly serious, if I may be permitted a poetic expression. It is through such paternal evidences of interest that we know, from time to time, that our state government intends to look after us. If the bill should pass, I predict that after the first hunting season, each surviving resident of Washington County will be driving a $5,000 automobile.

Never ask for
an apple.

THE ORIGINAL FORBIDDEN FRUIT WAS probably a kumquat or a shagbark. It couldn't have been an apple. The other day I was perambulating the periphery of my preserves, and I came around the end of a stone wall unexpectedly and saw some juvenile heels disappearing into the bushes. It was right where the Red Astrachan tree was shedding its ripened fruit like manna.

When God in His infinite wisdom set up the affairs of this world, for some reason He made the best apples the stealing apples. I think the literary aspects of the book of Genesis have overshadowed the author's deductions of fact. Stealing an apple is no crime.

It's time we looked at it for what it is—the un-

97

alienable right of children whose carefree feet take them at random over domains that are forever theirs. They cannot be proscribed, and they should not be. For purposes of civilized order we have to set an age when the right ceases, and I suppose twelve would be a convenient time. After twelve, a child no longer has to sneak around and steal apples. He can go to the door and ask for them, or he can buy some. But under twelve—I grant the right, and I was glad to see those heels skipping out of sight.

There, but for the years, went I. I had to laugh, of course, because there wasn't the slightest need for those heels to act as they did. I wouldn't have to think long to run down all the neighborhood's heels and decide which were which. Besides, all the youngsters know where my stealing apples grow, and they don't have to make a production out of getting a few. From time to time they all come walking in, in full sight, and help themselves. They know they can. In the winter, even, when they come to skate on our pond, they know they can go down cellar and get apples any time they want. There's no need of a boy's stealing apples. But boys continue to steal apples, and it is so openly a part of God's great plan that we're foolish to ignore it.

I have heard folks lament apple stealing, and have heard them say, "I'd give them all they want if they'd just come and ask." One fellow said,

"They deprive me of the fun of giving them some." Any boy knows that if he wants an apple he needs only to step into the first yard he comes to and say, "May I have an apple?"

The answer is going to be yes, because even if a farmer opposed the basic idea, he'd be so disarmed by the request he couldn't help himself. This might render all farmers generous old codgers, but it would eliminate the need to steal apples, so the whole idea is foolish. Any boy knows, anyway, that you never go into a yard and ask.

What you do is sneak in by the elms at the lower end of the orchard, crawl up along the wall on your hands and knees, and then find the best-equipped tree. You chew one on the spot, to support your choice, and then stuff your shirt full and get up and run. Once back on the road, you're safe. The farmer, if he sees any of this, has to play along, and most of them have a particularly nasty way of saying, "Get out of there!" This makes the whole thing valid, and the apples always taste a good deal better.

It's true that stealing apples are the best apples. The Red Astrachan, Transparent with its watercore, Strawberry St. Lawrence, August Sweet— apples like that are far and away the best apples of all. You can't pick them and ship them to distant markets and a handsome price. They mush too soon, and bruise too easily. The handsome Minister Apple, finest of all apples to steal, isn't ripe until it drops, and an hour after it drops it isn't any good. You have to be there in that precise hour, and then you get something worth stealing. A Red Astrachan is like those delectable vintages whose goodness is circumscribed geographically—ship them beyond their native valleys and they die. Take a common apple like a Northern Spy or a McIntosh Red, and they are better if they come to your hand chilled from a just-right cellar. But a Red Astrachan wants the warmth of an August sun on it, and carrying it even half-way home will spoil it. It's a small-boy's apple, made to fit his pants pocket and his growing mouth—where sometimes the teeth are not yet distributed with equal regularity. An Astrachan can be construed as a nice apple for a toothless customer. It makes a good friend to take up the brook fishing, and from time begun the youngster and his dog who try the brook in August have gone first to the moist earth by the sinkspout to dig worms, and then to the neighbor's Red Astrachan tree to get nourishment for the trip.

A boy would look funny going around to ask if he might have a Red Astrachan. It doesn't work out, and I can prove it. Once I was stealing Minister Apples, and Ruel Hanscome stood in the barn door with a grin on his face that obscured the hat on the back of his head, and he yelled, "If you want apples, why'n't you come and ask?" So a couple of days later I went and asked him for an apple, and he gave me a peck bag of Minister Apples which I carried home after eating a couple. Mother didn't seem to understand this too well. I don't remember that she wept, but I think she felt I was losing my mind. We had four Minister Apple trees in our own yard, under which the ground was littered with perfect Minister Apples, and my arrival with a peck from Ruel's didn't improve my intellectual standing about the house.

I can tell you, too, that God opposes any overt effort to stop boys from stealing apples. One time Grandfather had a fine crop of Duchess apples on a large tree near the road, and as they neared maturity he feared for his profit. He did an unethical thing, and it was displeasing in the sight of the Lord. Gramp took about a dozen beehives down and set them in a circle around that tree. Gramp was quite a beekeeper in his day, and he knew that while some boys mightn't be afraid of the bees, the presence of the hives might cut down the attendance somewhat. He was right, for the apples expanded and their bright and striped color adorned the sky without any inroads from the neighborhood children. One day he went amongst his insects with a ladder and gathered a big cartload of Duchess apples, which he sold in the village at a good price. He was delighted at his acumen.

But the unalienable right of small boys to steal

apples proved to be out of Grandfather's hands. One day right after that he and the hired man were teaming some cordwood up, and they had a big load on. Grandfather was sitting up on the load and the hired man was holding the reins and also driving. The horses had to strain to get the load up the hill, and were going at a good clip as they approached said Duchess apple tree.

The hired man pulled gently on the nigh rein to turn the horses into the roadway, and the leather pulled apart. This left the hired man with only the off line connecting him with the trend of events, and as Grandfather's hired men were never engaged for their intellectual capacities it was a moment fraught with great potential. The hired man jerked on the single line and made some coarse remark which deeply offended the team. The team responded by trotting off briskly in a great circle. This circle, by the obvious intervention of the God of all apple stealing, turned out to be exactly the circle in which Grandfather had set his beehives. On the first tour of this circle the careening equipage merely flattened the hives and left them a dismal coagulation of shards and comb.

This did not please the bees, and rather than join in the errant humor of the moment, they took umbrage and arose to let the world know how they felt about it. The umbrage of a bee is quite hot.

102

God wasn't mad at the horses, so they didn't get stung enough to cause them to hesitate in their headlong, if circular, flight, and they kept on going around and around, largely because the hired man kept pulling on the one rein and yelling. By this time Grandfather started to yell, and neighbors up and down the valley said they could hear every word just as plain, and that if they had been the hired man they would have been sore. The hired man actually was sore, and as he tried to force his mind into a reasonable facsimile of a function, he slacked off enough on the rein so the horses widened their circle a bit and finally went under another tree, the limbs of which combed Grandfather and the hired man off the load and dropped them to the ground, bees and all.

The horses then stopped running in a circle, and ran in a straight line up to Peppermint Corner, where they went into a barn owned by a Polish man who was not expecting them.

Grandfather could see that the whole thing was retribution, and he was pretty tolerant after that about boys and apples.

Another thing about stealing apples is the bothersome truth that you can't steal them from yourself. When we went out in groups and decided to steal apples, we would always arrive in due time at our place, and I would stand out in the road and wait while the boys went in and stole

Ministers. Each boy in turn would wait in like fashion when we swiped from his home grounds. Also, if you want good apples, watch and see where the boys steal the most. We had all the orchards and all the varieties catalogued, and you didn't catch us stealing inferior fruit.

Well, that view of the heels disappearing reassured me that some things in this world continue to be all right. They're still poaching, and as long as we have children and apples, I think the primordial prank will go on. I simply think that original tree in the blissful garden was something else besides an apple—maybe a peach or a quince. It couldn't have been an apple, because God would have understood stealing one of them. After all, He knew that poor Adam never had a boyhood.

🏵 🏵 🏵

You'd never know
it was there.

AT LAST I HAVE FOUND A CHANCE to speak well of picnics. I have always claimed they are evidence of social maladjustment and unnecessary among well-balanced people. But I have been convinced they serve a purpose. Possibly you, too, have friends who like the open, or frank, type of cheese.

Heretofore, the only good picnic we ever had

got rained out. I was delighted. We got all ready to go, and were just about to pack the baskets out when it began to pour. So we went in the living room with our baskets, kindled a cozy fire on the hearth, and had a picnic. We toasted weenies and burned marshmallows and dripped pickle brine on our pants and one chap was lucky enough to catch a glass of milk in his shoe. Everything was lovely.

This time we had no such good fortune. The sun shone and looked a good deal bigger than was necessary. A few friends from the village came with their hampers, and I saw it was useless to hope. I went on ahead and kindled a fire and got things ready, and shortly the merry company arrived, all talking at once, and demonstrated a festive mood.

They rode up in the new trailer. It is painted a picnic red and bounces just uncomfortably enough to be the thing for a picnic. A young lady with a red playsuit and rose-colored glasses drove the tractor, and was able to find all of the bumps in our woodroad. With shrieks of glee they arrived, and scarcely anybody was maimed or disfigured.

Our picnic spot is a lovely place—on a knoll under some ancient red oaks. I have laid up a fireplace complete with grill, pot-hangers, and sticks to spear into hot dogs. I have distributed planks around which older folks can sit on and younger folks can fall over. Surrounded by heavy woods, the spot is ideal because a child can wander off and get lost in any direction almost at once. When city people come to picnic with us, I feign as if looking about for a moose. This is very effective. I also tell how the bears wait in the fringe of the forest, and after we have gone come to forage for taffy papers, watermelon rinds, and similar picnic by-products. About once a summer somebody will fail to doubt me quite enough, and when little Velma disappears and I suggest perhaps she has been swallowed up by the interminable forest, the mother's shriek is joy to my ears. It is barely possible I have conveyed the idea that I much prefer to sit with my feet under my own kitchen table and eat that way.

This picnic was about like any, including the arrival of a hearty participant who had brought a supply of strange things to eat, which he began to force on everybody else. I don't know why people do that. I will eat my oatmeal for breakfast in any company, and never try to shove some down nearby throats. It is the same with apple pie. But when a person likes the self-advertising brands of cheese, he becomes a public nuisance by demanding that everybody within gunshot eat some with him. I like certain cheeses, and within due bounds will perform heroically. But when they attain a stigma, and cast a gloom over the whole township, I find I can get along without them and

106

not feel I am denying my palate anything to speak of. If I am ever accused of murder, it will be because somebody has found a profferer of rotten cheese with his head bashed in, but so far I have conducted myself well in such encounters and have stayed my temper. I have felt, somehow, that if the cheese wouldn't kill him, nothing would. There is a futility to resistance.

This man had a whole basket of goodies, and when he lifted the cover I thought some one of the kiddies had just come from stirring under the outhouse. The gleam in this gentleman's eye, however, soon led me along the right path, and I steeled myself for what came next. Shortly he was going about the happy picnic circle with a daub of his best discovery yet on the end of a knife, inviting everybody to smell, and to have a little. Some of the women paled and hurried into the bushes, and a deaf old fellow up back trying to get a cap off a beer bottle got wind of it and said, "Excuse me."

The best way to cope with one of these cheese artists is to hold out a cracker and let him deposit a sample on it, and then dawdle over a pickle until he has gone away, after which you can kick up a little place with your toe and bury the whole business. Thinking to do this, I held out a paper plate and received my sample. But the man didn't go away. He stood there and kept saying, "Eat it, go ahead, try it, it's delicious, try it." So I kind of had to try it, and at this moment I found out what a picnic is good for.

I took a frankfurter and speared it on a stick, and held it over the fire until the rigor mortis had been dispelled, after which I inserted it in a hot dog roll. Previous to inserting the frankfurter, I had lined the cavity with mustard, chopped onions, piccalilli, and pepper relish. On top of the frankfurter I tastefully deposited the cheese my kind friend had donated, and he beamed with satisfaction when he saw I shouldn't get away from him this time.

On top of the affair I erected three stuffed olives, a section of cucumber well salted, and a length of dill pickle. I then added some more relish and a dollop of mustard, and finished off the top with some split radishes, for color. I then ate it.

The truth is that I never knew the cheese was there. Folks sat in amazement and watched me down the thing. The cheese man, highly elated, then went around the circle again, insisting everybody have a good big slug, because they could all see with what evident enjoyment I had downed my sample.

For me, I had a perfect out—I just said, "No more, thanks—no, no, I've had enough to eat."

Which was true. But there was one picnic I kind of liked.

❀ ❀ ❀

Your author essays
   a poetic piece.

AT THE PRESENT TIME WE HAVE
no poet laureate on Lisbon Ridge, and I am filling
in until a candidate applies. It's a shame we
don't have several good poets here, because poetry
is just laying around for the picking up, and I
can't so much as pick up the eggs without seeing
a dozen chances for a ripping good jingle. We
used to have a poet laureate here, a real country
versifier who made out fine. His name was Moony
Tim Cluney, and he always said he was born with
a caul. The truth was that he was born under a
buffalo robe while his father was walloping a
horse trying to get Mrs. Cluney home from a
schoolhouse junket. Moony's background wasn't
what you would call prophetic, but as a poet he
was tops. He didn't have to worry about classical
forms, he just opened up and let go. His best
poem was a thing in which he rhymed "flute,
Annie" with hootnanny, but he often did things
that a lot of people thought were just as good.
He couldn't tell how his cows were milking without doing it in rhyme, and he certainly had the
soul of a poet.

Other than that the Muse's wings have seldom
brushed our happy neighborhood. Lacking anything better, I was kind of wishing Tim could
have been around this morning, because we had

a day for poetry, and it has simply gone to waste.

A lot of absurd things have been said off and on about our Maine weather, and I am willing to admit that there are spells when it isn't so good. But by and large we have about as good as anybody, and for my part I'm satisfied with it in every way. It runs along doing this and doing that, and we get a little of everything, and not enough of anything to create a habit. The days are lovely, and the sunsets are nice, and the easterlies fill you with awe, and the cold weather has its delights, and the cooling shower comes to chasten a hot August day. Maine people do a lot of talking about their weather because it amuses outsiders, but when you take a fellow out of the state and set him anywhere else in the world, he finds what weather means, and he's homesick. I always am when I get away.

But on top of that the Maine situation now and then sets up something a little extra, and when circumstances are right, and the portents jibe, we get an occasion that makes a poet essential. We may get two of them in a week, and then we may not have one for ten years. But when one of them hits, it's an occasion. And this particular morning that set me off this way was just such a time. It was the first day of December.

We'd just finished up a rainstorm. It was a nondescript kind of thing—a regular Maine rain. All the signs were against it, and the barometer was sky high. The rest of the country had been having some rippers, and our radios were telling about ten-foot drifts in Minnesota, and shipwrecks on the Great Lakes, and all such as that. We missed out, and our little rain was just the tag end of a disturbance that wasn't close enough for our local goosebones to bother with. The ground had thawed, a couple of inches of water lay on the pond ice, and something of a suggestion of spring was in the air. November went out with the touch of May, and we went to bed at a good Christian hour. Sunrise was due at 6.52, and as that is close to breakfast time we were up and about and found that the advertised time had been scrupulously adhered to.

Now, during the night this combination of weather happenstances had taken place. The wind did just so, the temperature touched exactly such-and-such, the humidity did precisely this, and all other conjunctions, oppositions, aspects and elongations were harmonious and congenial. This was the rare and unpredictable moment when the Maine weather cycle would hit the perfect moment—ending one period and beginning another.

It was precisely at sunrise. A plump and congenial sun came up to look things over. A heavy white frost covered everything. Not just the withered grass in the fields, but the entire vista from the window where I looked out over the orchard and saw the homes down the road, the trees, the walls, the forest on the distant hill.

Everything had a mistiness at first, and shapes then came out of the night. The fields found their borders and the woods learned where to stop. Down the road in a tie-up window a light came on, and for a minute or two the light was a thing by itself. Then the barn took shape, the light less prominent, and finally the light outside was equalized until the spot no longer shone.

The first red snatch of the sun set the whole scene to jingling with a ruby richness worth a whole canto to a real poet. But that was nothing. The conditions in nature made the sun stay red long after he has usually subsided his first splurge, and he came up into the sky with a redness nobody would believe unless he stood there to see it. The kitchen was red, blood-red, so the oatmeal steaming in the nappies was red, and the cream in the pitcher was red, and the cat washing her face by the range was the color of a fire engine that cost $15,000. I have a red shirt for wearing out around the dooryard when the hunters are in season, to distinguish me in their eyes from the antlered white-tail, and it is such a red as you would not want to live with day in and day out. It is a red which can stand up in a chair and shout and be heard for miles. But in the red of this December dawn my shirt was no more red than Mother's white ap'n—no more than the front of the white-enameled stove with the red muffins sitting in the red tin in the red oven door.

Then the sun climbed into the clear sky, and the thick frost on the world changed with it until the colors ran the range of precious gems. The red faded and there came an unbelievable blue—turquoise and amethyst, even a plain green-gray which was loveliness itself, and finally the color leveled off until the whole thing was merely the crystal clear brilliance of cut diamonds. As if it had rained diamonds and they lay a foot deep all around—crusted on the fence posts and grape vines and the roof of the barn.

Then the spell was broken, and this fortuitous moment in the conjunctivity of conditions had passed away. The thermometer rose to 34, then 36 and up to 40. The diamonds vanished. The dooryard changed back to gravel and gray grass. A wisp of mare's tail appeared in the sky and the whistle of a freight train down the valley echoed with the foreboding of weather on the make. It was over, and I knew that I might never again be precisely here when the Maine weather touches briefly on the perfect.

I was here all right for this time, and I'm glad —and lacking a real poet here on the Ridge to enshrine the spectacle in deathless words, I have merely done what I could in my own prosaic way.

Whether it be
more or less.

ONE TIME IN MY YOUTH I THOUGHT I would like to buy the Bar Harbor *Times*. I conferred with Arthur G. Staples, who was at that time the grand old man of Maine editors. His editorial page in the old Lewiston *Evening Journal* was an astute and literary contribution to our state's culture, and Arthur was a big toad in a little puddle who can rank, editorially, with anything our journalism has ever produced. Arthur said, "If I had my youth and pristine vigor, I'd buy it with you, and we'd raise hell."

Arthur and I computed the assets, with the publishing formula in mind, and decided the place was worth, at that time, about $5,000. This would include appurtenances and good will; spurs, dips and schists; and all possible likelihoods in every known direction. It was our idea that for the sake of a dicker, we might stretch a point and make it $6,000, but that was only if a poor widow was in great need, or they had a rare book collection or something like that.

I thereupon went to Bar Harbor and introduced myself to a man who operated a bank there whose incorporated purposes had become, as banks do, interested in the sale of the paper. This gentleman, who never did know a masthead from eodtf, fixed me with a $10,000 smile, and said to come in, that the Bar Harbor *Times* was definitely for sale, and that I had come to the right man. Entering his luxurious countinghouse, I lapsed into a soft armchair and said something about examining the books and assets. I was in my early twenties, and had already established myself in Maine journalism so there was no misgiving in my mind as to what went on with papers and printshops. I could "cost" 500 envelopes as well as the next man, and I knew that when circulation eased off on Spring Street, the thing to do was start a little agitation for sidewalks and better streetlights there. The Bar Harbor *Times* appealed to me because it had a fair local publishing field, and also had countless millions of summer wealth which I supposed, in my exuberance, the right man could tap in various helpful ways. The business venture of

$5,000 wasn't much in terms of smart publishing in that town, and I could have raised it at the time.

So this banker told me that he was ready to make the whole thing over to me for $42,000. He was even glad to be able to do this, and indicated the bank would have some stationery printed there now and then to show their faith in my ownership. It was a mutual affair—if I believed in them they would believe in me, and we should get along famously side by side in our respective business ventures. He said some more, but I did not hear him, because by that time I had applied my hat to my youthful brow, had gone out to my Model T, and had driven slowly off Mt. Desert Island and was half-way home. I did not hear the conclusion of his remarks. I smothered my sorrow at my failure to acquire that property, and reported to Arthur Staples shortly that I wasn't quite fool enough to become the James Gordon Bennett of Bar Harbor.

Subsequently, Editor Staples found out what the score was and we were both able to enhance our visions with the news. The bank had evidently loaned money to the newspaper's owner until his value to them had reached the aforementioned sum of $42,000. This sum had been secured by two things—the owner's unquestioned honesty, and the paper's material worth. The owner's honesty was as good as gold, and the paper was worth just about the $5,000 we thought. At this point the owner did a very unkind thing—he up and died. After death, mortal honesty is not negotiable. The Bar Harbor *Times,* percentagewise, immediately became the most valuable newspaper property in the world, before, then or since.

I have many times congratulated myself that the banker was so completely ignorant of the publishing formula. If he had known the slightest thing about the cycle of readership, circulation and advertising, he would have gladly sold me his hopped-up property at my figure, just to be shut of it, and I would today be what I would today not want to be—a Bar Harbor editor. Thus did the complications of financial affairs do me a favor, and I have often been seen while haying or weeding carrots or counting my pullets—leaping in the air and kicking my heels together three times and cheering just because that banker was so kind to me.

The matter did, however, fill me with the truth about banks and bankers, and I have had many thoughts on the subject. Not long ago our local bank ran a foreclosure notice in the paper, and thus came into possession of a piece of land just below us here on the road. The farm was never owned by our family, but Uncle Jacob had the place just above it, so Uncle Jacob's old line is cited in the notice as a boundary. The official wording runs, ". . . thence westerly along land of one Jacob Gould 140 rods . . ."

Uncle Jacob's farm never had a mortgage on it in his time, and he has been gone since Civil War days. His old line fence was put up back around 1800, and for a generation or two was tight. In later years the posts have gone, the wire has fallen and rusted away, or has been covered by pine needles as the forests took over the one-time clean fields. Uncle Jacob was a neat old fellow, and took his line fences seriously. They were straight, meticulously on the line, and extra-good for purposes of a deed. When the farm next below was described as lying along a fence of one Jacob Gould, there could be no question about feet and inches.

The bank has come into a dubious asset. The fellow who owned the farm in question mortgaged it to the hilt, and then stripped it. Every stick of lumber was cut off, the fields were cropped to their limit. Then the buildings started to fall in. The bank acquired the farm because the farmer intended they should. They thought they foreclosed, but he would tell you he sold it to them. And he would be nearer right.

Years ago things like that didn't happen so often. The local business field was understood by banks, and they cultivated prosperity and sound practice. Here in this area we had an old fellow who did most of his banking business from the seat of a buggy—he trotted out around the community looking for places to invest a few dollars at the customary 6%. Farmers didn't let their buildings fall in, because he helped them keep them up. He'd loan $299 for new sills under the barn, and return each interest date to keep his investment alive. He understood farming and farmers. The minute a note was paid off it was his job to find some other excuse to put out the money again. In a sense, he was doing his community a favor, but in a truer sense his community was doing him a favor by putting his dollars to work. Constant and close contact with his customers kept him informed of over-all business conditions. His caution in seeking adequate protection for his loans promoted sound values in town. You couldn't fool him into thinking a $2 pigpen was a sound risk at $599. When a newspaper in a town like Bar Harbor gets up to $42,000, there's something radically wrong with the entire fiber of the community. It isn't just ridiculous, it's unsound beyond fantasy. You've lost your buggy-seat attitudes.

When a bank comes into possession of a stripped farm, with the fields running to hardhack and wiregrass, and the barn roof down in the manure pit, there isn't half so much wrong with the farm as there is with the bank. Somewhere along the line a bank failed in its obligation to its community. Maybe the banker should have given his money out on small, short-term notes, rather than in a killing dose. Maybe he should have dropped in now and then to talk about the price spread on a dozen eggs, or to see if the heifer would freshen in May or August. Perhaps he should have used the influence of his institution to kill the Milk Control Act in the state legislature.

I think if I were a banker and had advanced $42,000 on a $5,000 asset, I should at least subscribe to *Editor & Publisher* and see if I could find out what an agate line is. I think knowing things like that would mitigate my great grief when I found out how wrong I had been.

On that old deed they ran in the foreclosure notice the phraseology was antique, but durable. It concluded, ". . . thence easterly along a line of said Gould to a corner of a fence near a pair of bars, and following an old fence along a steep bank to the road, thence along the roadway forty rods to point of beginning, containing eighty acres, be it the same whether it be more or less."

My observation would merely be that sometimes it isn't the same.

❦ ❦ ❦

People don't whittle
any more.

EVERYBODY IS THINKING UP new ways to save the world, and mine is to start whittling. People don't whittle any more. They don't know how to whittle. They don't even know what whittling is. Saving a world without whittlers by whittling may strike some folks as a dubious program, but it is exactly the kind of thing a whittler would understand. In fact, a whittler would understand all the other programs too, even if nobody else does.

Whittling is esoteric. When you get through you have a pile of shavings and chips, great peace of mind, and nothing else. It is not to be confused with wood carving, or any other occupational pastime. Making little balls that turn inside of a stick, boats in bottles, birchroot warclubs, or even peeling willow to make a walking stick—these things are not whittling. They result in something.

The whole trouble with everybody today is that they result in something. We would be better off to have a large portion of our population whittling, then we would not result in something quite so often, and we would be more relaxed as a people.

Whittling has no connection with the thought process. It runs with the grain of the woods you select, and when you have found out how the grain goes you can shut up your knife and arise to stride forth to more worldly things. A whittler lapses into a coma, so to speak, and almost anything can happen without disturbing him. He is relaxed, and is doing nothing. This is very different from "not doing anything."

The great difficulty of modern times lies in our

122

accepted belief that putting in one's time constitutes accomplishment. It's like Progressive Education, which holds that saying something in class is in itself a contribution. The world has got over the silly notion that saying something is a lot better if you have something to say. Also that doing something is far better if you have something to do, and do it. These modern concepts add dignity to a lot of talk and work that would not, to a whittler, look like much. The unskilled and craftless workman whose union dues are paid is willy-nilly drawing the wages paid for that machine, and because he is getting paid he has the notion that what he does is important.

No whittler would subscribe to that idea. When you whittle, you put in your time and your muscular exercise is noteworthy—but you don't dignify it by letting on that you're producing. The distinction is important. The whittler at least is honest. No frills about it. No putting on airs. In a world that is kidding itself, the whittler doesn't kid anybody. Doesn't try to. He can't even kid himself—which is the basis of all true knowledge and art. When a fellow begins to kid himself, things are in bad shape.

Today unemployment is often as gainful as working all day. For some people it is even more remunerative. We have a gentleman here in this town who never earned above $25 a week, but by combining various forms of social assistance, often at great personal sacrifice, he was able to whangle $325 a month out of the state welfare funds. This permitted him to sit around a good part of the time, and frequently his wife would have another child. This would be reported quickly to the state, and thus far has always turned out to be a lucrative arrangement. The man is able to spend a lot of his time whittling, and this tranquillity of spirit has permitted him to adopt a calm attitude toward life in the aggregate, and he makes out fine. The point being that only by whittling could this state of affairs be accepted so complacently. We don't know what the poor fellow would ever do if he couldn't whittle.

But this shows you how modern ideas can gum up the customs of the people. The art of true whittling thus becomes a kind of industrial therapy, and a fellow like me who supports his family by earning what they eat is reluctant to whittle, lest somebody think we're on the town. With a man whittling for $325 a month, the taint of commercialism has settled upon our art, and there is no longer any point in whittling for nothing.

If you don't whittle for nothing, you are not whittling at all. To whittle, you want a good stick, a sharp knife, and the ability to withdraw temporarily from the world and all things therein contained. Not as a permanent profession, but temporarily—with every intention of snapping

124

your knife to and going back to work when the time comes. For the time being you don't care if school keeps or not. The end result is nothing more than a pile of shavings—nothing more.

This purposeless application may or may not be accompanied by thoughts, but it is better not to think. The world has plenty of thinkers who can keep us in hot water without spoiling a good stick of whittling wood. A true whittler never glamorizes his nonproductive hiatus with high-sounding euphemisms, never excuses himself with false claims of therapy, or resting, or trying to keep his hands busy while he works out a problem. He just whittles, take it or leave it. Complete, resigned indifference.

The present world can't grasp this at all. The elimination of utility is unthinkable. You have to be doing something—even day beds are functional. If you happen to be doing nothing, and get caught at it, you jump up and rationalize the thing. The whole field of psychiatry is based on man's desire to let on he's doing something when he ain't. Diplomacy is the art of saying something nobody can hear, or hearing something nobody said. Men who have daily attended their sweatshop positions, and have done nothing for weeks more strenuous than wearing their clothes will hire a man to phrase their inactivity into high-sounding grievances. This is the way we are. Today, if you should see a true whittler indulging a few moments, you would naturally ask him, "What are you doing?"

That's all a modern observer could think of to say. It would force the whittler to say, "Whittling." The modern observer would thereupon have to inquire, "Yes, but what are you making?"

So the world is away beyond the point where my suggestion will cut any ice. I know enough not to ask a whittler any such fool question. The proper thing for the observer to do is whip out his knife and look around for a stick, and try to find out what happens to a man when he whittles.

He ceases to be. No hungry generations tread him down. He is one with the infinite and eternal. Peace and immunity descend upon him. He encompasses all the universal complacency of the meditative Buddha, without having his feet in such an impossible position. It is the true and perfect state.

Meantime every woe and distress is visited upon an unhappy world by meddling men who did something when they might have been whittling. If we picked whittlers for our legislators, soldiers, philosophers, teachers, diplomats—the world would be what we wish it were.

I have never known a whittler who wasn't agreeable, but the world is full of scoundrels who can't tell pine from cedar. I will promise and guarantee peace in our time, and for all time, if you'll just find some way to produce a whittler every time there's a public opening.

❦ ❦ ❦

What color is your lamb stew?

THEY HELD A MEETING OF painters and decorators up to Poland Spring the other day, and an expert got up and said color in the home is very important. He said carefully composed color would make for marital happiness and would cut down on the divorce rate. This sounds good.

I remember Dr. Plummer, debating something in town meeting once, said that an expert is a man with something to sell, so this color panacea turns out to be the Pittsburgh glass people, who are pushing tinted glass for the home environment.

So I have decided to say something about color in the home. I am in favor of it. I have color in my kitchen, tastefully arranged in a pleasing combination. I don't know what color it is, but I know it is color. I could get up and go out and look, but I recently had a hearty supper and I am quite comfortable where I am, and I hesitate to visit upon myself any athletic exercise over and above the essential. It may be on the yellow, but I think it is pinkish. Whatever it is, it is a nice color, and has contributed largely to my happy home life, which is at this time satisfactory and felicitous.

The color of a well-cooked supper tends to unite husband and wife in one happy bond, and while gaily tinted plates with sentimental scenes may enhance the occasion, a good white plate will serve just as well if the roast beef be done properly and the boiled onions have enough butter on them. The color of good food is a symbol of love and good. Two fried eggs, accompanied by a properly tinted slice of ham and some browned potatoes are a fine thing to adorn a kitchen, and can be improved somewhat by a properly pastelled sheet of johnny cake. Hubby will forget all about hunting up a lawyer, and Mother will lean back and relax in the sweet sound of his encomium. The divorce rate would collapse to nothing if the delicious color of a juicy raspberry pie could be worked into the kitchen motif about twice a week.

I didn't go to that meeting, but I think the glass blowers are limited. Any good cook could make cathedral windows look plain and drab if she extended herself. And the doting husband wouldn't care what color his sidewalls are if he could feast his eyes wantonly upon suitably frequent occasions and a lamb stew, both at the same time. The artistic appearance of a well-made lamb stew, with plenty of moisture around it, might well make lovers of fine glass inattentive for the nonce.

After a hearty meal a kitchen is brightened up a good deal by the effect of a chocolate pudding capped with whipped cream, on which a cherry has been delicately seated by a loving hand. I doubt if the particular shade, tint and hue of a well-baked custard pie could be properly imitated in glass. If it came to a choice between neatly colored Pittsburgh glass and a pan of hot buttermilk biscuits, I should hate to have all my money in glass stock. I like my kitchen colored with the rich darkness of thick molasses to run on freshly tinted home-baked bread; the joyous harlequin of cookies and cakes and boiled dinners and cross-barred peach pies and brownbread and cranberry jelly and floating islands and buckwheat cakes and ever and anon the delicate marine hues of a haddock chowder.

Glass colors never smell.

My colors smell good, and they make me purr and shine. My home life is better for them. Daddy no longer plays the horses, and Sonny stays home from the pool halls. Sisters hang around Mummies to learn the receets, and the boy friends come for supper—and I mean supper. Mother, of course, hums magnificently. She doesn't have time to

129

grouse, thinking about new ways to add color to the home and thus entice further compliments.

Glass colors are all right as far as they go. So is a lamb stew, but I think it goes farther. It has such a delicate nuance the second day.

Where are the snows
of yesteryear?

THE CHANCES ARE I WON'T get far on this one, because too many years have gone into the reputation enjoyed by Maine winters. The rest of the world has the idea that whenever the temperature ranges above zero we consider it warm and open some windows to change the air. This is our own fault. We go around saying, "Oh, no—we don't have much snow, only 15 or 20 feet. It's the drifts that bother." Then everybody laughs, and goes around telling about the rigors of the Maine climate.

We used to have winters, but something has happened. I wish that statement might be accepted, but it won't be. People hear it, and sug-

131

gest maybe the Gulf Stream has veered. They think maybe we're going to tell them we've tipped the state up so the sun's rays hit us straight on. I don't know what's happened. I just know it has. February comes and we haven't had any snow, the fields are bare and the pond is slushy on top. Ski clubs go out of business. The highway commission has a brand new problem, consisting of frost-heaves because of the lack of snow covering.

And all the time people think we're just buried, and have the windows nailed shut with blankets tacked over them.

The difficulty in forwarding belief in the truth is complicated because true Maine people, led by habit, continue to tell how the bride got her train tangled up in her snowshoes, and our nature poets sing of frost like diamonds and the cold, clear, cutting wind at the tie-up door. If anybody from Maine ever opened his head and said we were having warmer weather than the famous sun resorts a hoot of laughter would go up. Actually it's true. A letter from friends in New Orleans tells how the Mardi Gras time was a flop on account of the cold, and another friend in Atlanta grouses about below zero weather. We haven't been below zero all winter.

That doesn't mean we haven't been below zero in the past, and it doesn't mean we may never again—but we haven't been this year and the sun

132

is already over the barn gable and maple trees are about to be tapped.

A few years back the little town of Rangeley was isolated for weeks when a blizzard dropped yards of snow onto the down-state highway. It was inconvenient, but it didn't work any hardships on anybody, and in those bleak days it was passed off as the regular thing. Then the folks at Rangeley with rooms to let got the idea of making their lovely region into the East's leading snow resort. They chipped in 50¢ apiece and bought a bottle so they could hold an organization meeting, at which they elected a committee and drew up some by-laws. It was a good meeting, and everybody felt good about the prospects of another at an early date. They ran up a ski tow, and got a big engine to run it. They began to promote their facilities and had everything fixed so when one man had filled all his rooms he could shunt further inquiries on to his associates. They got in touch with the Maine Development Commission and were promised the customary high grade of interest in the general plan, although they could not endorse it specifically because other places with ski tows might not like it. Everything was all set.

Rangeley hasn't had any snow since. If you want to go skiing, Carolina is a better bet, but Western Pennsylvania is running ski tows off oil well engines. The Carolina people don't think it will last.

Then the Rumford Winter Carnival began having trouble with the weather. The chill winds wouldn't co-operate, and there came a time when the annual snowshoe race was run off in the gymnasium, and they had to bring in snow from New Hampshire for the ski jumps. The New Hampshire snow was all right, but the trucking expense was bothersome. They still hold the carnival every year, and have quite a program, but the children come in summertime playsuits, and one year the ladies all rushed home to close the upstairs windows during a thunder shower.

Down at Camden they had a thing called the Snow Bowl, but after a few seasons when they had hardly enough snow to fill a nappie the thing lost some of its wallop, and they took to considering a country dance festival as an alternative program.

And this is absolute fact—where the farmers used to team great loads of logs out of the woods on runners, using horses and oxen, modern trucks go in and get stuck in the wintertime mud. Of late years the bigger lumbering outfits have brought in track-tractors, and keep them standing by to extricate trucks.

There used to be a woman who lived in the Big Island Pond camp of the Megantic Fish & Game Club all winter, as a caretaker, and people used to marvel that she would ski twenty-eight miles down to Eustis for a week end in town. They marveled,

134

because that was snowshoe country, and anybody on skis was considered a sissy. The very idea of making a sport out of the rigors of a Maine winter was ridiculous, and they used to kid this woman for making the trip the hard way. Well, last year she came down the last week end in January, and used a bicycle. And let us not forget that this region is high up on the Height of Land, just this side of Canada, at a point where Benedict Arnold lost so many men during the hazards of plain October weather.

Maine people really like winters. During these past few inadequate winters the common cry is, "I wish it would snow—we'd all feel better if it would only snow." But it hasn't snowed. The weather makes up, just as it used to in the long ago, and then the wind hauls southerly, it warms up, and we get a warm, gentle rain that soothes the landscape and brings out pussy willows and pansies and dandelions. On February 25, 1951, Larry Poulin of Lisbon Village caught a moth flying around. It was one of those things that lays eggs on tomato plants. That's no way to have things.

One thing people ought to know is that the old-fashioned Maine winter was a time of sunshine and beauty. It was cold, and we had our ways of meeting that. But the days were beautiful. Official government figures record that the sun shines more hours in Maine winters than it does in the highly advertised resort sections to the south and west. A Maine winter day is a lovely thing, and should not be dismissed too readily. We have times when the fireside is your best bet even yet, but the snappiest days of an old-time winter were good days and Maine people liked to get out in them. When the moon was fulling, and deep snow stood on everything, and your boots creaked on the dooryard snow, it was wonderful to get out for a coast on the hill, and people did. You could even excuse a sleigh ride, such nights would be so pretty.

But those things are gone.

Once it was custom to stand a broom by the door, so visitors could brush the snow from their feet before they tracked it into the kitchen. Now they lay down a clump of evergreen brush, so visitors can scrub the mud off their shoes.

The old poet * who made paean about the rarity of a day in June was right on his toes as far as winter went back in those times. But if he asked the question now of any State of Mainer, the answer would be, "About any day in January."

That's about the size of it, and I'm only reporting this because it's so.

* Jim Lowell.

✿ ✿ ✿

You've got to be
pretty smart.

Now THEY TELL US THAT RADIO-
isotopes will increase farm production. Nuclear
fission marches on, and the cheering fission farmer
will be right there with his profits up and atomic
words on his smiling lips. The present excitement
appears to center about the usefulness of radio-
activity as a tracer through the organisms of plants
and animals. Thus we can understand plant life
and nutrition as soon as we have mastered the
general fund of knowledge about the universe
around us. In other words, the Massachusetts Institute of Technology will be the best place to
find out if you should put three or four seeds in
a hill.

I'm against it. Not that it isn't so—no doubt
it is so. I will believe anything that will further
the public weal. I'm against it because it's too
hard for me. I am still trying to understand about
summer scald, and not ready yet to expand into
more complicated fields.

Summer scald is caused by cold winters.

That is, it really isn't, but a person who has
other things on his mind and wants to get away
in time to bowl a couple of strings with the boys
will do well to accept that and be content. When
somebody asks you what causes summer scald,
you just say, "Cold weather," and they may avoid

137

you for a couple of weeks, but your answer can be sustained by a few hours' work with the orchard bulletins and your county agent.

Those of us who grow a few apples have to show some interest in these things, however, and when we dig into the summer scald story it gets a little involved and we don't jump up and shout so loudly when we hear of radioisotopes. A farmer, today, is a man who hears that summer scald is caused by cold winters, and he never bats an eye.

Of course, there are complications. One of them is boron deficiency, which is cured by Epsom salts. My father dropped in to pay his respects one afternoon when we were unloading a shipment of Epsom salts for the orchards, and thought somebody was sick. He shuddered to think what that quantity suggested, and kept wagging his head as he watched us pile the 100-pound sacks in the barn. But we were taking boron deficiency very seriously in those days, and poked it right to the trees in good shape.

Another complication is magnesium deficiency, and the best feature of this is that there are 27 other things you can't tell it from. A good cure is Epsom salts. Now, there may be some who administer borax for boron deficiency, and this is all right, too. Because if you don't cure the boron trouble, you will be working on the magnesium, and the truth is that neither one of these things is a cause anyway.

I don't want to get complicated about this at this time. I realize these pages are perused mostly by non-bucolic people, and that the general population isn't equal to the complicated conversations of the farm hand, whose every act has been elevated into a stiff intellectual exercise by the experts. You may notice that I said "administer" borax. In the old days we used to "spread" stuff, or "put it around." But today everything is administered, including ten cents' worth of borax. Let us proceed:

The only thing that ails your tree is lack of potash. I think it's potash. It's either potash or potassium carbonate, I can't remember which. But you can pile potash (or potassium carbonate) around your tree ten feet deep if you want to, and it won't do a bit of good. You will be wasting your time.

As I understand it, what you do is put on some Epsom salts. This gives the tree magnesium. Nobody ever explained that to me, and I can't at this time hazard a guess. The Epsom salts are more of a decoy than anything else, and after the tree gets enough magnesium in this way, the potash ups and takes care of itself. I don't know where the potash comes from, and I never found anybody who did.

Now, summer scald, or magnesium deficiency, is thus characterized as a secondary reaction, and has no separate being. It is a symptom, sort of, but unrelated. The leaves turn yellow and drop off along in August. But it is now too late to do anything about it—you should have applied Epsom salts back in the spring.

I might say that winter scald is another matter, and is caused by injury to the cambian layer by excessive warm weather in the latter part of the dormant season, followed by frost. There is nothing you can do about that at this time, but we are working on it as fast as the experts can look up big words.

Actually, my explanation of the thing, here, is lucidity itself, and while it may call for several readings by the uninitiated, the meaning will be readily mastered by any farmer with no more than a glance. It is all a question of nutrients. In essence, the idea is that if you want potash, you apply magnesium; if you want borax, you apply miscible oil and camomile. To be a successful orchardist you always do something else.

The thing breaks down into the assimilation of nutriments. If you want a good tree, make it assimilate a lot of nutriments, and you can't go wrong.

Now, the reason I have explained this so carefully is on account of this sudden appearance of isotopes. As I understand it, the isotope is to a crop what Epsom salts are to potash. You will never get any tomatoes by planting on a good forkful of isotopes, but you will be able to find out what it was you should have put under the tomato plant instead. This will be very helpful, and will result in forward progress of incalculable value. The radioisotopes are like the third-base coach, who doesn't play in the game himself, but has to be on his toes every minute. I quote from the official release: "Radiocalcium is utilized (not *used*, mind you, but *utilized*) in the study of effects of application of lime to the soil. . . . Research with radiophosphorus and radiochlorine is expected to yield important knowledge of absorption of phosphate and chlorine from the soil." You see?

Agricultural effort has thus been diverted from the strenuous course we first followed. If the carrots aren't doing too well, you weed the beets. For every ailment there is an equal and opposite remedy. For potash, you read magnesium; for lime you read calcium. The thing may eventually reach the confused stage where you can't tell what will come up just because you planted corn. We may yet hear of the man who dug his cucumbers and threshed his potatoes. The atomic age has merely begun, and who knows what wonderful things lie ahead?

I'm still opposed to it. I was a happy man, once. I could arise in the morning with no more problem than which side of the bed to use, and I could look off into the glorious east and admire the beauty and majesty of dawn without breaking the display down into isotopes and nutrients.

I would like to remain at peace with my destiny. I do not wish to plant isotopes and grow utilizations. I would like to stay where I am—with nothing but Epsom salts and borax on my mind. To continue blissfully in my easeful and simple manner, wherein food problems consist largely of whether to boil one turnip or two. In my condition nutrients are unknown, and I swallow my breakfast mostly because it will last me until dinnertime. I want to stop with magnesium deficiency, and go no farther. That's far enough. Beyond that, madness and the age of fission.

I do not wish to radiorubidiumize my farm. It suits me the way it is. I just want to grow a few things, and put down enough for winter. If they are stunted, and puny, and scalded, and runted, and chock-a-block full of deficiencies—I'll love them just the same.

❦ ❦ ❦

*Continuity is worth
    something.*

ONE DAY I TOOK MY FATHER A present. It was a curio for his collection. I said, "I want you to have something real old—something your father's father's father made when he was a small boy." Dad certainly was surprised.

He didn't know what it was, at first, but now it has an honored place among his curios and he gets it down when people call and has them guess what it is. Dad's curios are worth seeing, really. He has a petrified snowball. He has other things equally disturbing, such as a box full of holes in case somebody wants to make a cribbage board, and a doorknob that came off in his hand when he called on the governor. And now he has this new thing.

Some of Dad's curios are less spectacular. He has the top of a skull that came out of an Indian graveyard in the Bad Lands, and fossilized clamshells they dug from the mountains of Montana. And so on. There's a petrified vertebra joint from a prehistoric animal. Enough so an hour can be spent with his junk and not considered wasted. The other things are thrown in to astonish people.

Well, what I gave him was a straight-grained piece of maple with a hole in it. The hole was made by one of our ancestors when he tapped a maple tree long-long ago to make maple syrup. There is no authentic way to compute the time, but nobody has ever tapped our trees except the family, and any holes in them belong to us.

The maples in our sugar grove can't live forever, and every once in a while one of them will give up. The wind may break out the top, sometimes lightning does it. All at once I find myself addressing a tree that is bigger than I am, and apologizing for the rudeness of cutting it down. The family has established wonderful relations with these trees, and whenever one is taken down we feel the loss of a friend, and also observe the relentless pulsing of Time, because we're all getting on together. Sugar maple trees make excellent firewood. But they do come hard. Anybody working alone, as I do, takes his time and doesn't measure the day by the number of cords piled up. Running a one-man cross-cut saw down through the butt-log of a four-foot maple is not frivolous amusement. You work. Then you have to bring the steel wedges, and a 16-pound maul, and sliver off your firewood piece by piece. Nowadays anybody can get a power chain-saw, and if anybody were cutting firewood for profit he would. But my woodcraft isn't all business, and I still tackle a tree now and then in the pioneer fashion. I'm not in any hurry, and there isn't anything else going on during the winter, and it's nice up in the woods, and the old tree has to be cleaned up, so easy does it.

I make a kind of an outing of it. I take a lunch in a basket, plenty of apples, and plan to spend the day. I build me a little fire against an old stump close by, scraping away the snow, and have a good bed of coals glowing by noontime. The fire is also used to keep the frost out of the wedges, because when they get too cold you can't make them stay in the cleft. If they are real cold, they'll sometimes pop out of the log and scoot into a snowbank fifteen feet away. Many a time I've misjudged the temper of my wedges, and spent an hour digging for them in a woods snowbank. There are also hours when I don't cut much wood for other reasons—maybe I just want to sit on the stump and watch a couple of red squirrels chase each other.

Something a lot of people don't realize, nowadays, is how easy it is to keep wood on hand for fuel. Everybody speaks of cutting wood as if it were one of the labors of Hercules, and only the extremely dull-witted would ever cut any. That's not so. The best tool for cutting wood is a congenial disposition. If you like to get out in the open, and can bring yourself to face something besides golf and angling and admit that cutting wood, too, is exercise, I think you'll find it will provide as much athletic delight as you will need. My contention is that it serves every purpose of skiing, and when you get through you have a pile of wood instead of a broken leg. Anyway, I like to take my time frittering around the woodlot on a good winter's day, and while I never try to set any production records, I do keep ahead of the woodbox.

So this day I started on an ancient maple that had lost its top in a storm some years back, and had gone past any service to our spring sapping operations. This one had long harbored a swarm of wild bees in a cleft far up the trunk, and for some time I'd meant to cut it down in an October. I didn't get to it and the bees winterkilled in the meantime. I didn't do the job all in one day, of course, but one morning I had the wedges warmed a little and set about splitting out the big trunk.

When our pioneer ancestors came up here from the coast, this back ridge of ours was covered with hardwood growth. The maples, beech and oak stood so close together you could walk along putting hand to hand on the trunks. Great solid trees, every one. In the years since the oaks and beech have been cut out and to some extent the maples have come to old age without replenishing themselves too well. The number steadily declines. This is mostly because the woodland cycles run from hardwood to softwood, and man is too short-lived to survive the full circle. But we still have plenty of maples for our sugaring.

Each year, then, somebody in our family has gone the rounds of these trees, boring holes into the maples and inserting the little spouts. In the earliest days they bored big holes with shipwright's augers—the kinds used to treenail timbers—and stuck in whittled spouts made from old-growth pine. Later the metal spouts came along, and they dropped down to $\frac{7}{16}$th inch bits. But year in and year out each of the years produced a new hole. And each year the wound in the tree was left to grow over. As the bark expanded and the holes were covered, the butt-log of this particular tree I was working on kept a secret record of every springtime. And when I drove in the wedges I laid this record bare.

So I cut out one of the holes nearest the heart of the maple, split away a squared piece of wood, and got a strip of wood with a hole through it. That's what I took to my father. The hole came just right so he could hang the piece on a peg in his den.

I told him which tree it came from, "It's the one just below the spring, by the rock with the garnets in it." Dad knew just which one it was. I said, "That hole was bored by your grandfather when he was about 25 years old."

Dad said, "You could have found one that I bored when I was about the same age."

I said, "I could have found one I bored when I was about the same age."

I could have found, out nearer the bark, one my youngster bored within the past few years—a succession of generations that, I think, adds a lot to our life here on the old family place. I had quite a time tapping trees that spring, the first spring the lad helped, because he wanted to bore all the holes, and his size was against him. It held us up a lot. It takes a lot of strength to put tap holes in a whole woodlot of trees. But, of course,

147

a youngster has to start sometime, and if he's anything like the rest of the generations he'll someday have a lad of his own up there to add one more round of tappings to the old trees. I kind of hope . . .

*I don't know anything
about goats.*

Beyond the fact that the
British Navy finally decided goats cause Malta
Fever, I have slight information on the subject,
and am glad. But goats always interested me on
the question of whatever becomes of them, anyway? This is one of the wonders of our time, and
we shouldn't dismiss it without full investigation.

The goaty fraternity follows an interesting pattern, and I have always suspected there is a society
of goaters. They must have a magazine which
promulgates the faith, from which goaters can
memorize set speeches to forward the movement.
A man, for instance, will be proceeding happily
along life's meandering path, taking his wife to
the movies with uxorial regularity, seeing that the

149

children make progress in their education, and all at once he runs into the goat story. The hallowed light of a crusader then kindles his moist eye, and he is a goater.

The points are interesting: Goats are easy to take care of, and when you go away you can carry her on the running board—thus keeping your supply of milk uninterrupted. The goat is handy, and can be kept in an old box if you lack more sumptuous facilities. They are convenient, and all they need is a box to stand on while you milk her. They are good for pets, and are kindly. The milk is healthy and nourishing, and fetches as much as 35¢ a quart, and even more. And so on, but they run about the same every time, and in the end each new convert has a flock of goats and handles them with a kind of religious fervor. He grasps every chance to forward the goaty movement, and will snatch at any opportunity to take over the discussion. I heard a man, once, say, "Well, the kids kind of raised hell around the neighborhood Halloween, didn't they?" And at this a goater burst in, "Speaking of kids, I was reading in the Goat Journal that . . ."

But after a time some kind of reaction sets in, and then one day the goater is chasing around trying to find something to do with his goats. He still quotes the twenty-five incontrovertible reasons, and insists that goats, next to Christianity, are the leading salvation of our muddled world.

150

But all the same, he would like to sell some goats, reasonable. His manner suggests that he has undivided loyalty, that he knows full well how fine goats are, but that out of the goodness of his heart he wants to add to human welfare, and desires to take you into the glad company of goaters for your own good. It's like getting a bid to join the golf club.

This goes on all the time. Everybody who gets goats is shortly running around trying to un-get them, and after it is all over there is a noticeable shortage of hircine anatomy in the meat markets. This is (a) something to think about, or (b) something not to think about. Any lady who purchases a fine roast of lamb in the butcher shop and then finds it is not up to the high standards of former times, may well wonder what has happened to her neighbor's goats.

A goater on his way out will stoop to any chicanery to effect his purpose. One time we felt grain was too high, and we sold off our cows until things settled down. We either had to sell the cows or give up our yachts and shooting lodges. So we began buying milk, and a goater heard of it and descended upon me. He proposed that what I needed was a couple of good goats, that they would supply me with all the milk I needed. He recited all the speeches, telling about the 35¢ a quart, and all we needed was to get down on our knees and pray together.

151

But his arguments availed naught. I am goat-proof. So the man pulled his trump card, and appealed to my sentiment. He wrung a bitter tear from his sorrowful eye, and said that if I wouldn't buy these two goats, he would just have to take them to the butcher. For his part, he said, it was just like parting from his dear old mother, but there was a limit to how many goats a man could keep, and he was surfeited to the point of drastic action. (I found out afterward these were the only goats he had, so he was speaking the truth.) Controlling my anguish, I told him he had better go to the slaughterhouse, then, and I walked with him to his automobile. I was afraid his grief was so great he might collapse in my dooryard. But he manfully reached his vehicle, and I found he had the two goats in the back seat. I also found they were both wethers. This is a scientific word, and perhaps not in the vocabulary of non-rural people, but among other things it means that the beast will give damned little milk, at least not right away. I told the man he was a crook and a fraud, whereupon he swallowed his sadness and laughed, and said it was worth a try, anyway. He went to the slaughterhouse and the cruel deed was done, but I couldn't find any goat meat in our local markets afterward.

My observation of goats has always been at a distance, and I notice that they are aloof, and will get away up on the woodshed roof to avoid people.

This permits him to disseminate his goaty aroma to a more receptive atmosphere, and a good goat can be highly successful this way. The goat is not, however, the gastronomically promiscuous creature commonly shown in the newspaper cartoons chewing on an old tin can. Goats will not eat tin cans. The truth is that they are extremely fussy about what they will eat, and a goater is hard put at times to find choice fare for their jaded palates. You give a cow a forkful of old swamp fog, and she'll pick it over and get something from it. But give a goat the finest sweet meadow clover, and she'll be insulted because you handled it. Now and then we sell a little hay to goaters. At first we cracked our product up the way we will when it's going for cows and horses. But we found out the goater has to have samples first, to see if his animals will touch the stuff. It may have been cut on June 21st instead of June 22nd, and therefore useless for goats. If the goat shows interest, the man will come back and buy a bagful. He won't dare to take more, because tomorrow the goat may feel like another kind. Then he tries to pay for it with goat milk. The gustatorial versatility of the goat is a myth and a joke.

The story on goat milk is largely a myth, too. It will, indeed, fetch 35¢ or 40¢ a quart, providing you can find somebody to buy it. According to the set speeches this is easy to do, because it is so nice for folks with bad stomachs and other ali-

153

mentary ailments, and every hospital and sana-torium is eager to meet the goater. This gives you a clientele with one foot in the grave, to begin with, but the new goater seems to find that this market is already sewed up by other goaters.

The goaters have always tried to tell me how easy it is to milk one. They simply stand up on a box, and in a trice you have done the job. This is much better than a cow, who couldn't stand on a box anyway, and will sometimes dally along until she fills an 18-quart pail twice a day. As much as I hate to milk, a goat doesn't appeal to me that way. I have a dog that we don't have to milk at all, and that suits me, but if I've got to go through the maneuver anyway, I might as well have a Holstein. Keeping a milch creature just because you don't have to milk her much is a left-handed way of getting a problem solved. Be-sides, I heard of a goater who drank goat milk all the time, and because he worried so much about extricating himself from the society he developed ulcers.

As to the odor of goats, I would never keep one for that reason. You can get much the same effect from a good sheep, you don't have to milk the sheep, and once a year you can clip her and get some wool. A goat will make all the atmos-phere a sheep can, and even more, but the wool isn't worth clipping.

154

I don't wish to deny the goat any civil liberties. I am willing to be friendly, and I will believe in goats if they will believe in me. But I do wonder, as things move along, just what becomes of old goats. They spend a lot of time trading and trafficking, and they must end up somewhere. Beef, pork and lamb seem to have an arrival, ultimately, on the meat block, but the tawny old goat, with his rich, ripe, penetrating experiences, seems to vanish away, softly and suddenly, and never is heard from again.

I don't care, but I do wonder about it quite a good deal.

🏵 🏵 🏵

*Let us set this
record straight.*

It says here in this magazine that an Indian named Quadequina brought a bushel of popped popcorn to the Pilgrims for Thanksgiving in 1630, and that popcorn is now a major American industry. This is good. But the story doesn't tell me how Quadequina popped the stuff, and it's something I've always wanted to know about. Ever since I was in grade school I have heard it said at intervals that the Indians taught the Pilgrims how to pop corn, and until just now nobody has ever told me how the Indians popped it. Why is it that nobody except me ever worries about these things?

One evening long ago Grandfather and I were munching corn in the old farmhouse, and he started off on the old-old story of the Indian. It wasn't the first time I'd heard it. Gramp said the Indian never carried a packsack of grub on his trails—he took a little bag of popcorn. No need to weight yourself down. Travel light and eat hearty. A handful of popcorn, a fire—and you've got a hearty meal. I lifted my youthful face, aglow with the thirst for knowledge, and asked Grampie how the Indians popped it.

Grampie looked at me, indicating he hadn't ever thought of that, and suggested it was bedtime. Always after that, whenever he was yanking the big sheet-metal popper back and forth over the red-hot top of the Queen Atlantic, he would wag his head. He never figured it out. It was one of the few times the old fellow didn't have an answer for me, and couldn't advance my knowledge to some extent. It has always been a moot question.

The simple children of the forest must have had some method of converting the kernels into full-fashioned fare. How did Quadequina do it? There were no tin-plate and woven-wire utensils in the dim beginnings of North American popcorn culture, and if the Indian had something else to tame his jumping maize, it would make an interesting contribution to what we know of these forest people—particularly if it was a device he could sack off with him on his vagrant trails, bent either on personal business or pleasure.

I used to picture the agile brave leaping about in a rod circumference around a hot rock, chasing down his popping corn before Adjidaumo beat him to it. Retrieving corn that way would take off fat quicker than corn would put it on, and the legends in our family never told of a brave that agile or that active. The Indians our family told about would rather go hungry than exercise so strenuously.

And I've never had any luck picturing the Indian with a corn popper—any kind. I can't seem to visualize him treading the forest path, his moccasins lightly touching the velvet moss, a bunny-skin of popcorn at his belt, his bow and arrow at the ready, and a popcorn popper caught up under his nether arm. It just doesn't work—I can't see it.

There is no record I know of where an Indian, confused in the excitement of a massacre, forgets which hand his tommyhawk is in, and bops a surprised pioneer behind the ear with a long-handled popcorn popper. I think that would have happened, and there are plenty of stories to suggest it might have. Down at Potts's Point in 1654 an Indian was surprised by a volley of musketry from the Holbrook henhouse, and he tossed his paddle aside and began to make his canoe go with a

157

flitch of bacon—a natural reversal under such circumstances. So I don't believe an Indian ever had
a popcorn popper, or we'd have known about it.

Nor did they have a substitute. We folks can
take an iron spider, cover it, and make a popcorn
popper just as good as a real one. But the Indians
didn't have any such things. A good many settlers
got along without things like that, too. In our
family they were fed heartily for years with no
utensil except a big copper kettle. They cooked
a good many things with no more equipment than
the Indians had.

The Indians knew how to cook many things,
but none was as explosively elusive as popcorn.
They heated rocks and broiled lobsters and clams
on them. They hung strips of meat in the smoke
of the tepee, and they rolled fish and birds in blue
clay and cracked off the brick when they were
done. A handful of popcorn inside a mud pack
would probably have led pristine Indians to
believe they had discovered the atomic bomb
before its time. But the Indians didn't discover it,
and they remained crude and primitive in their
culinary accomplishments right up to the last
minute.

I suppose the hot flat rock is the best bet, and
one the general public will readily accept as the
Indian's most likely mode of popping corn. He
built a fire on a flat rock, and after the rock had
soaked up all the heat it could stand the Indian

158

brushed off the coals and strewed his popcorn. This is good. I am willing to grant this might pop the corn, all right. But see how! The air is full of flying kernels, and there goes the Indian looking through the junipers, sweetfern, hardhack, alders, hackmatack and blueberry bushes with hopes of recovering enough to ward off starvation. It takes quite a while to hunt down a meal, and by that time the rock has cooled off, night is coming on, and we are agreed that is no way to sustain yourself in the uncharted wilderness.

If Quadequina had a bushel of popcorn for Thanksgiving at Plymouth, he must have been a-popping of it since April. But year in and year out we are handed the claim that the Indians popped corn, and nobody has ever answered my question. I still can't figure out how they popped it.

Well, a story in the papers said Congress devoted the first few hours of their meeting to handshaking. They certainly had just the crowd for it, but what I wanted to do was show you how far off the beam you were on that business of the Indians and popcorn. You ask somebody how the Indians went about the business of popping corn, just as I did here, and immediately he begins to think up ways in which it might have been done. Some of these ways are magnificently ingenious, and we wonder if the Indian was quite that smart.

159

What really happens in this little intellectual exercise is that everybody makes an error in logic—he assumes that the unproved minor premise has been incontrovertibly established. Everybody assumes that the Indian had popcorn to pop. From the angle of simple high school debating, this is a bad way to start—you lick yourself before the game is begun. If the Indian, truthfully, never had any popcorn anyway, why spend all this time figuring out how he popped it? See what I've done to you? Just because you didn't pause in the very beginning and analyze your problem, and figure out where you were. Let that be a lesson to you.

Evidently you don't have any of that basic Yankee disinclination which my friend J. Bixler calls "logical positivism," or which Josh Billings called "it may rain, may not." It's the old white horse routine—one man says the horse yonder is white, his logically positive friend answers, "Well, it appears to be from this side." You don't jump at conclusions. You don't become a fanatic for homogenized milk until you learn what it is. You don't have the Indian jumping around a hot rock after popped popcorn until you establish if he had any to pop. It's a case of drawing your reasoning powers off to a fine point, and being ready at any time to resist the pressure of unproved information. In fact, the question of primitive culinary accomplishment among the American Indians is

160

no longer half so important as the present consideration of how far we were beguiled by a quack premise.

Well, what happened is that one day I asked a certain fellow how he figured the Indians popped corn. He gave me a curious glance, and instead of going off into hypothetical presumptions the way everybody else had, he asked, "What makes you think the Indians popped corn?" Logical positivism was at work.

I said that there was an article in *Reader's Digest* that told about Quadequina bringing a bushel of popped corn to the Pilgrims. This fellow merely said that *Reader's Digest* might be in error, which hadn't occurred to me up to that point, and which may, after all, be possible.

Anyway, this fellow said that the Indians had corn. Not only have the histories said so, but by word-of-mouth reports in his own family he feels safe in accepting that to begin with. He told about relatives away back who had been on Swan Island and had seen the Indians growing corn, and had eaten with them both at the Island and on the trails. They told their children, and so the story came to him and he felt safe in believing it. Corn. But not popcorn.

"When I was a sprout, but old enough to remember," he told me, "I went with my sister Nan over to the farm on Clam Hoe Hill where Aunt Prue

161

was living. She was an old lady then, and I suppose we were about ten and eight. Anyway, she went back into Indian times, and while we were there she said she'd fix us some corn the way the Indians ate it. Not popcorn, mind you, but corn.

"So she laid some kernels of plain yellow corn, what we called horse corn—the field corn . . . Not sweetcorn and not popcorn, just plain corn. So she laid the kernels out on top of the stove and made what she called parched corn. It didn't pop. It didn't snap out across the room. But it did break open and swell up, and she picked it off the top of the stove as fast as it broke open. She had about a cupful of it when she got through, and she stirred in some butter, and we kids sat up straight in the old kitchen chairs and ate it. It was good, too. And according to what Aunt Prue said, that was the way the Indians took their corn whenever they approached popping it. That knocks a hole in your handsome hope that the Indians had popcorn poppers—but it's not the first time unfounded arguments have been demolished, so to speak."

So now we know the difference between parched corn and popped corn, and we can see how wrong it is to jump to unwarranted conclusions. The next time somebody asks you to cogitate on step two before anybody has demonstrated step one—don't be so willing to co-operate. It's a strange thing when you can get the American Indian all rigged out with a corn popper away back before anybody had perfected popcorn.

❦❦❦

As you sow, you
reap so-so

SOME STRANGE KIND OF A CLIQUE has the obsession of planting seeds all over everything in an effort to gladden the fading landscape. I was reading about it somewhere, and got quite worked up. These birds do such things as lean out of railway trains and scatter seeds along the right of way, under the impression that people to come after will be delighted at the lovely prospect. If ever I saw a scheme predicated on causing trouble, that's it.

I want to do what I can to dissuade this group of do-gooders from doing too much good, because this kind of uncontrolled propagation might soon have us in a fix.

Controlling the variegated vegetation of nature is the farmer's only real problem. Millions of dollars are spent each year making things grow, but every effort in a positive way is offset by much greater effort negatively. Wheat is a splendid crop, but you don't want any alfalfa in it. Anything that doesn't belong is a weed, even if it serves at an-

163

other time and in another place as a useful plant in itself. How would you like it if you tilled your acres year after year, gradually eliminating unwanted weeds, and just as you got your piece of buckwheat started you saw a woman driving along the road sprinkling a bag of blue vetch seed right where it could become mighty pretty in your field?

If I could catch one of these seedsters at it, and convict her in the court of public opinion, I think I have a suitable punishment in mind. It would be to take a ten-barrel crop of kidney beans, and go through them and pick out all the yellow eyes among them caused by a thick-headed hired man who forgot to clean out the planter before he started a new field. A person who has faced that necessity in order to get top price at the village store is a great hand, in after seasons, to look in the seed chamber of the planter and make sure.

I suppose it's easy to see how this cult got started. They decided flowers were nice, and decided to do what they could. Strewing a few pounds of double hollyhock seed along the Union Pacific right of way would seem like a fine thing. It might occur to them that in time the train would howl through the countryside between palisades of magnificent blooms, and that passengers to come later would cheer at the foresight of the seed casters.

Somebody must have told them about Johnny Appleseed. Somebody has told a lot of people about Johnny Appleseed, but nobody ever told me how they got good apples afterward. If you want a bitter disappointment, you plant the seed from a nice apple and then wait until it produces fruit. The somewhat technical subject of cross-pollens among apples has never been an integral part of the Johnny Appleseed yarn, and I've often wondered about it. To get good apples, you graft, you don't sow. I'd like to know how Johnny Appleseed overcame that stiff condition of nature; and if he never did, then his part of the country must have some terrible apples.

Well, with the flower seeds there are also objections. Some seeds are bound to fall on stony ground, to begin with, and some among thorns. But I've tried to grow some flowers time after time, and never got anything. We planted a whole flower garden one year with all manner of lovely things, but all we got was a castor oil plant that grew ten feet high. We gave up and turned the plot into grass, and the next year had a fine bed of horseradish which is still abounding and fructifying so you wouldn't believe it. One of the queerest things I ever heard of about flower seeds has to do with Great-grandmother's poppies. Long ago she built herself a posy patch by the meadow wall, just this side of the upper orchard, and for several years she had a wonderful batch of flowers. They say it was beautiful, tastefully arranged and a riot of color. Then in the cycle of doings the

165

meadow got laid down to wheat, and then it went into hay, and time ran out for Great-grandmother. But ever since then, whenever that field is turned over, her poppies reappear. They were a small scarlet poppy, fragile and dainty, and they wilted with the rising sun and had their brief moment in time. It went to seed, but it never came up again in Great-grandmother's day: Its glory was as brief as a glint, and then it lay dormant for years. Now, when the field is turned over every dozen years or so, the poppies leap up and gaze about to see how times have changed. About twice in a generation our family sees Great-grammie's poppies. They do no particular harm, but I remember how mad Grandfather was one morning to find them in his clover. It just made the clover look silly. And I suppose they'll be there, time without end—waiting patiently for those occasional years when somebody plows that field.

I can see how farmers are going to feel the same way about seeds dropped from railroad windows. A Kansas farmer will find salpiglossis in his wheat, and soundly curse the 5.56 eastbound. Perennial pennyroyal will come up among Cape Cod cranberries, and there will be weeping at Hanson. Creeping lazy-lucy in the corn and painted candytuft in the onions will vex the rural population, and all the while the peripatetic seedsters will be lecturing to their Friday club meetings on the great strides made in beautifying the country.

166

I can't help wondering how the Lawnsdale Garden Club will like it when some farmer, sufficiently vexed, retaliates by tossing a good dose of Hungarian Millet in the petunias and zinnias. A well-ordered flower garden is a laudable ornament, and a fine achievement. Much study goes into the subject, and a lady with a watering pot and a red-handled trowel is no doubt a boon. It is merely a curiosity of fate that she will get mad at finding a few shoots of silage corn in her coreopsis, but will shortly entrain for Indianapolis and toss salpiglossis seeds among the soybeans en route.

After hundreds of years of careful grooming, British gardeners are said to offer a guinea to anybody who finds a weed in their bent. That would be a good time for somebody to start promulgating the theory of random scattering of strange and unrelated flora. Perhaps these traveling tillers should converse with grain growers who get charged 5¢ a bag for cleaning mustard from the oats. They might ask why somebody invented a device so you can cut dandelions from your lawn without stooping over. Or, they might consider the hours upon fatiguing hours spent by farmers who drag spring-tine harrows back and forth endlessly across their fields to tear out the penetrating roots of the ubiquitous witchgrass. That would be a good time for a transient landscape artist to whip out a bag of assorted seeds and let go.

It's just plain no good. Grandfather used to plant

some flowers among his vegetables now and then, but he did it because he wanted them there. He used to say he spent most of the summer among his crops, and that's where he had to have his flowers if he was going to see them. But flowers and vegetables grew together with equal control—he knew what he was doing. He'd have been awful mad if somebody else did it for him.

So if you see some crusading lady leaning out the window of a cross-country bus, and she is beautifying the roadside with an assortment of nasturtiums, phlox, marigolds, morning-glories and columbine—you tap her on the shoulder and tell her if she wants to plant something that I've got ten acres she can sow to lespedesia. I'll even let her spread the manure.

And if she doesn't show any interest in this useful offer, then push her out, seeds and all, on the next curve.

*It doesn't matter
when you vote.*

EVERY BIENNIAL SESSION OF THE Maine legislature, there's a Democrat who wants to change the date of the Maine elections. Every two years he gets slapped down by Republicans only because he's a Democrat. But I'm glad, because I think he's got the wrong idea. As a state we have spent millions in advertising and promoting the natural resources, and in some instances have done rather well. And for the price of one extra election, we get a free story on the front page of every American newspaper once every two years, with customary observation that as Maine goes, so goes . . .

We couldn't buy that space at any price, and if

we voted when other states do we'd have to share the space with 47 other competing sponsors. The September date of the Maine State Election is therefore cheap advertising, and even a Democrat ought to realize that. However, one aspect of the matter that has never had attention is the question of what Maine does on that crucial day in November when all the other states are holding their biennial elections. I shall relate what went on here the last time to occupy the attention of the citizens.

About dusk the night before, Monday, two young hunters returned bug-eyed from the vicinity of the Shine Fortin farm and said they had seen a thing. They were clearly in the throes of tremendous excitement, and were heavily armed with high-powered deer rifles. It is noteworthy that neither had made any attempt to shoot this thing, but it was felt their agitation was probably so great that they had momentarily forgotten their guns. The thing, they said, was about four feet long with a tail of good size, brownish in color, and it had a shrieking wail that would make a pot boil at 200 yards. The boys told the right people about this, and then they went home to supper.

Mrs. Fortin said that she didn't doubt it for a minute. She said they had been having trouble all summer to get their cows down in the far end of the pasture, and some months before they had concluded there must be some reason for this. At

170

first they thought it might be the dry season and the consequent dropping off in provender, but now it was perfectly clear that the cows had been afraid of the thing. Mr. Fortin seemed pleased to have attention thus focused on his acres, and he said he was quite sure he had seen the thing himself. He wasn't too sure of some of the other distinguishments, but the thing did have, he said, a tail about like that.

The question of a tail is of great importance. Maine has wildcats, known as bobcats, which are completely harmless to humans but will occasionally tackle poultry and stock. When they do, a good dog and a gun is the best answer, and many of them are shot each year. But a bobcat has no tail. But years ago Maine had another kind of a wildcat, the longer tailed and longer legged Canadian lynx, which was slaughtered by the colonists because of its predatory nature. As far as Maine is concerned the lynx is either extinct or so much so that he might just as well be.

The French in Canada called this lynx the loup-cervier, or lucivee, and invented stories about him even taller than the ones he thought up himself. In real life the lucivee was a sturdy character, and nobody loved him. One time Will Andrews caught one in a deadfall and tossed the carcass in his canoe, after which he poled out in the stream and began to shoot the Skedibook white-water. During this exciting three-mile run the lucivee recov-

171

ered his senses in the forward end of the canoe, and Mr. Andrews is credited with one of the most remarkable feats of navigation in the history of the state. But over and above such actual occurrences, the lucivee has contributed well to legend and lore, and every agile-minded Maine man has done his best in a supporting role. It is customary, on any proper occasion, to spit to loo'ard and opine that a lucivee has no doubt wandered down from Canada and is on the prowl. At times this keeps the evenings from being too dull.

Now one of nature's most curious sounds is that of the lovelorn porcupine sitting in a tall tree discussing his philosophy with his equally lovelorn mate. Few people, being lovelorn, would enjoy being a porcupine at the same time, and the sound a porcupine makes while in this condition is easily mistaken for about anything, including a prolonged wail of pain from some unhappy denizen of the nether world. The love call of the hedgehog greatly aids in keeping the lucivee myth alive.

There are, too, other sounds in the stilly night which help. An owl discussing the perversity of the season is not incompatible with what a lucivee ought to sound like, in the minds of some people. And when a loon lets rip far down the lake with his hideous midnight clarion call, signifying that his mate is nesting and the eggs are hot, any helpful Maine native will tilt his head knowingly and say, "Must be a lucivee about."

So on what was Election Eve in the other states, the news went around here that a lucivee had been seen within the town bounds, and the menfolks were stirred to action. A posse of about 20, armed to the teeth with their deer guns, accompanied by dogs and carrying lights, assembled to go into the woods and rid the section of this crittur.

Now in spite of its great popularity throughout Maine, night hunting is illegal except for the raccoon, for whom you may hunt after dark with guns of .22 caliber only. It was therefore startling to see so many men equipped, including jacklights, on such sudden notice, but in fairness to them it must be noted that they paused to consider well their situation. They decided it was better to be sure, so they telephoned to Stillman Johnson, a game warden, and asked if it was all right to go out at this hour with lights and seek the lucivee. Johnson must have been sleepy, or the suddenness of the query caught him off guard, because he said yes—to go ahead. The posse thereupon struck out in good faith, although nobody seemed to notice that the two youthful hunters who had reported the varmint didn't go with them.

At about this time the safari was given a curious dignity by the arrival on the scene of William Knox, State Police trooper, who wanted to see a lucivee too. He was attracted by the great many stories that bloomed back in the settlement after the men had struck out. Somebody said the Jordan poultry farm had been cleaned right out by the crittur. This was not so. Somebody said a horse had had his side raked right down by the lynx. This was also not so. A Holstein bull had been carried right off in one piece. The next day it turned out that none of these things was so, but on Election Eve the people were in a mood to believe anything and efforts at substantiation were small.

Women were afraid to step out and get their dish towels off the line to finish up their supper dishes. There was talk of postponing public functions, and attendance at the pictures that night was hardly enough to pay the operator. So Officer Knox didn't want to miss anything, and he arrived in full uniform, side-armed, and his two-way radio system turned on to keep the outside world informed. It didn't occur to Officer Knox that a state-sworn officer was duty bound to arrest anybody he found in the woods with a gun and lamp at night.

But Warden Johnson by this time had come to. He hesitated to approach the posse with warrants, seeing as he'd just told them it was all right, but he did notify the press that it was against the law to hunt at night. He said he thought the men were just talking about hunting a lucivee in the daytime, but he didn't enlarge on why the lights happened to be mentioned. Anyway, he covered him-

174

self without spoiling the fun, and the posse was allowed to pursue the lucivee full tilt.

The posse didn't happen to find him. Shortly one of the dogs learned a 'coon had passed that way, and in a twinkling the pack was three miles away over the Ferry Road by the Allie Hatch home, with a 'coon up a tree. At this the posse adjourned as such, and re-formed itself as a committee of the whole. Members hurried home and swapped their deer guns for .22's, and shortly arrived over at Allie's as 'coon hunters. One of the Soychak boys climbed the tree and shook out the 'coon, and the matter was discussed from all angles by the dogs and men. He was a big fellow, but no lucivee.

So about the time ballot clerks out in the other states were opening the polls and spreading the check lists, our lucivee hunt broke up and went home with one raccoon and hearty appetites. After heavy breakfasts of meat and potatoes and pie, the several mighty men engaged in this great gesture in behalf of public safety went to bed and slept wonderfully. Possibly they dreamt of tufted ears and tails about so long, bounding through the puckerbrush seeking what could be devoured. Or possibly of wailing ear-piercing shrieks like a couple of lovelorn porcupines bespeaking their amours on the topmost limb of a forest giant.

But during the next day, which was Election Day out in the other states, our woods were crowded

175

with hunters hoping to find the lucivee asleep in a tree. All day they hunted, and when the polls closed they went home satisfied that things would be all right now. Possibly they felt it may, after all, have been a couple of porcupines.

Thus we spent Election Day in Maine, and although the hunting was good, we didn't catch anything.

The same thing, no doubt, can be said for some of the states that spent the day at the polls.

🏵 🏵 🏵

We had an awful
  good time.

OUT BACK OF THE BARN ON A knoll I have a log cabin, to which I retire at times and talk to myself. I find this is stimulating, because I am never interrupted or disputed by inferior intellects. So one winter when my family went to Boston for what they called a vacation I retired to my cabin, stoked up the fires, and began to labor on an imperishable treatise about a fish I caught once that could play the guitar. In this condition I was surprised by Saunders, the artist whose delineations of my emaciated features continue to please thousands. Mr. Saunders had sent his wife off on a vacation, too, and he had come to show me a bottle which he had picked up on the beach, and which he wished me to arrange for him in a still life group akimbo.

At that moment it began to snow.

Mr. Saunders and I were snowed in for three days, and we had a nice time. I wrote breezy little articles without number, some of which were afterward published, and every time I finished one Mr. Saunders would draw a picture to go with it. When we got through I had two articles without pictures, and he had two pictures without articles, so we came out even and did well.

I am a good cook, and we had the plentiful farm supplies to draw on. Ever and anon we would arise from our cultural pursuits and prepare some interesting dish to sustain us. Such as the lamb chops, hunter style. I would like to speak of these in particular, and I want to recommend them to any housewife who feels her husband may be drifting away. They are simple to prepare, and fun to eat. For two people, we found it takes thirty-six chops.

First you run a sharp knife about the bone, removing same and casting it into a pot for a stew at a later time. The meat comes off in such way you can roll it up like a section of jelly roll. Then you wrap a long strip of sugar-cured bacon around it, like a ribbon, and fasten it in place with a skewer. The chops are then laid out on an old-fashioned biscuit tin and thrust into an oven to see what happens.

177

A number of incidentals may be provided to accompany the chops when they are done, such as potatoes, turnip, squash, boiled onions, greens, salad and pie. The only strict essential is an acreage of corn bread, for which I always use my own recipe. (Copies are for sale to bonded applicants at $50 each, postage prepaid.) Thus Mr. Saunders and I continued to endure the vexing incarceration brought on by the storm, and by occasional snowshoe trips to the house, a hundred yards away, we were able to find varying comestibles to tempt our palates and sustain the bare minimum of life. One strawberry shortcake that I made looked so good we ate it for the main course, and kept the steak for dessert. So it went, and the storm raged without and piled up drifts. We knew not cark nor care, and permitted it to snow with unrelenting application.

Then somewhere along the line I discovered my rat was still there. I had a rat who lived in the cabin for many years. At times he would be the only rat on the farm, because I got all the others, one way or another. But this one outwitted me every time. He stayed on and on. Meantime, I fought rats in general with great success. Besides cats I have used other methods, including a 25¢ can of government rodenticide every fall. I put this around the orchards, and it works. In the fall I put random ears down under the corn crib, and watch until a rat has taken them. Then I put down some more ears, and after a time the rats are convinced that I am a generous man and worthy of their continued support. Then one day I put down some ears that have been treated with *Quelle Surprise!* Then I put down some new ears to see if the rat cometh again in the stilly night, but usually he appeareth to be more seldom.

Rats like what they haven't got. They'll riddle apples at random, but go all to pieces over a piece of salt fish. So I hang a piece of fish up on a string, and set a steel trap under it. This is quite a rig, and while unknowing witnesses might accuse me of cruelty, it is only because they have never been as mad as I get when I find what a rat has done to the apples. This is the common steel trap used for fur animals. I set it up on a box, and attach the chain so when it dangles the trap is still off the ground. The piece of fish wafts its sea breeze about the place, and presently attracts a nice rat.

What happens is important, and neutralizes the wickedness of being so hard on the rat. The rat comes and tries to get the fish. All he can do is cuff it, and it swings about on the string. Then the rat jumps for it, and as he is jumping the pan of the trap perceives a wonderful opportunity. The rat, finding himself locked in something he hadn't expected, leaps off the box, trap and all, and presently is hanging head down in mid air. Thus, neither going nor coming, he is paying the toll on his depredations. To appreciate the artful cunning

179

of this kind of trap arrangement, you have to know what the rat does next.

He squeals.

He squeals so that the farmer, two floors above and sound asleep, comes leaping out of bed onto the cold floor barefooted, and thinks the front portal of Hell has just opened under his bed and the assembled damned of all eras are arranged like a glee club and are serenading him in their immortal anguish.

The farmer instantly realized that this is waking fancy, and that the noise is really a trapped rat in the cellar, so he goes down and slaps the rat with a shovel and renders him inarticulate, after which he goes back to bed and sleeps just as if nothing had happened. A farmer seldom weeps when he murders a rat.

But the squeal the rat let out is the real reason for using that type trap in that fashion. Rats for miles around heard the squeal, and they immediately deduced that all was not 100% hunkeydory. They will go forty miles and fare badly on mediocre fodder rather than come into your cellar and run the risk of what happened to poor old Pete. They don't know just exactly what it was that happened to him, but they know he didn't like it. One good squeal like that will keep rats away for months.

So, you see, I'm no stranger to the job of fetching rats, but I still couldn't get that big one in the cabin. I set traps, laid out bait, and locked up a cat over night. But nothing was any good. I still had the rat, and while Saunders and I were doing our author-artist duet this rat made his presence known. He came into a partition behind the china cupboard and began to chew on something. It sounded like somebody dropping dry beans into a tin barrel, and Mr. Saunders looked up and asked me if I was all right.

"Yeah," I said. "It's a rat in the wall."

Mr. Saunders, I could see, wasn't going to allow this affair to pass at face value. He laid down one of his comet-hair brushes and asked, "What's he doing?"

I really didn't know. I have never known what rats in the wall do when they sound like a tuba player who has stumbled over the percussion section while taking his seat in Symphony Hall. This rat had been going into this partition for years and making this noise, and I had often wondered what he was doing. But I did not know. It was a good deal like banging oil drums with a peen hammer. He may have been gnashing his teeth, assuming he was good at it.

Upon a sudden impulse I arose and took the .30-30 rifle down from its pegs, slipped in a soft-nosed cartridge, and brought the butt to my shoulder. I took good aim between a teacup and a luster pitcher and squeezed the trigger. I then put the rifle back on its pegs, and Mr. Saunders came out from under the bed, one foot encased in a majolica antique I had hidden away, and he said that if I ever did anything like that again he would kill me.

The echo of the shot resounded back and forth inside the cabin for quite a time, and conversations were difficult. I brought a hammer and took down the partition wall and recovered what was left of my tenant rat. I had neatly severed his head and had blown it out through a hole in the log wall, in such a way that it was dissipated in the snowy night and was no longer serviceable. Mr. Saunders said By George, that was a wonderful shot and he could only commend my marksmanship in the highest fashion. I said, "What?" and he said By George that was a wonderful shot and he could only commend my marksmanship in the highest fashion. That is the only time I ever shot a .30-30 in a confined area.

My only purpose in relating this extraordinary account is to show graphically that it is not wise to interrupt cultural activities. If you chance to find an author and an artist sitting down together to produce lovely things, you should pass by on the other side and get to hell out of there.

❀ ❀ ❀

He said he enjoyed
every minute.

THERE'S A FELLOW DOWN IN
New York named Earl Wilson who says he's a
writer, and he was up here once gathering material for a book. This is a good place, all right,
and he made out. Some of our happiest hours are
spent with people who come up here to get something to write about, so we were glad to hear Earl
was coming. Doc Rockwell told us about it.

Doc is that retired amazement of the effete stage
who retired to Southport to write a book, and is
still working on it. It isn't exactly the same book
all the time, but he keeps changing it to suit the
meanderings of the era. When the atomic age was
announced he began all over again, and has 750
words done already on the atom bomb, to be
titled, "Here It Comes, Boys—Under the Bed!"
Doc continues to divide his time with many other
interests, and it wouldn't be fair to infer that he
does nothing but write a book. He also lobsters,
and sometimes catches one. He also continues his
well-established business of making fine cigar
ashes, and is Maine's leading student of the public
supper.

It was only natural that we should take Mr.
Wilson to a supper to enhance his knowledge and
give him something to write about. Doc looked over
the possibilities, and couldn't find a supper listed

183

on that particular evening, so he telephoned to us and wanted to know if we could lend a hand in this emergency. We certainly could. The church at South West Bend was raising money for a new furnace, and the supper they had scheduled for that very evening was promising. A furnace was at that time an important matter for the church, and they weren't going to put on any second-rate performance for such an essential matter.

This church is one of those old community affairs derived from the colonial beginnings of New England. In its earlier days the New England church was often more civic than spiritual, and it was hard to tell where pew rent left off and highway improvement began. The parish trustees were in possession of all church property, and if they wanted to convert the meeting house to a blacksmith shop, they seemingly had that right. So at some time in the history of South West Bend the church had become a town hall, and folks in the neighborhood pursuing any spiritual interests had to go elsewhere. But in recent years they decided to go back to holding church services, and shortly they found that the furnace in their ancient building was inadequate.

It was so inadequate that the Christmas service was held in utter cold, and the ice cream they served to the children in the vestry around a tree served to warm everybody up after the ordeal. The furnace supper was the next event of importance, so Doc and Earl and I showed up to assist in this worthy cause.

To Doc and me the aroma of the place betokened a successful evening, but we felt Earl was a little skeptical. When the supper committee took 50¢ apiece from me, we could see that Earl was doubtful. No doubt he thought he'd have to hurry back to Toots Shor's to piecen out; back to some accredited place where they not only charged you a decent price, but where 50¢ wouldn't even pay for laundering the napkin.

What napkin?

Earl tried to be gay. We put him at the head of a 35-foot table where the famished citizens of South West Bend were preparing their customary assault on food. There were a couple of fattish people in the group, but mostly they were the seemingly emaciated Yankee characters who look as if they never had a decent meal, but who actually are in slim trim. Upon suitable notification to God Almighty that the slaughter was about to commence, these citizens fell to, and somebody passed Earl a bowl of nicely browned kidney beans in which, because he was company, the crusted salt pork was still lounging on top. Earl daintily tried this offering, and from then on it was nip and tuck.

The citizens of South West Bend acknowledged an appetite when they saw it, and they got arm-weary passing things to the visiting writer from

185

the United States. The waitress, who was Maxine Herling, hovered over Earl and brought him things the others missed. He held a bean out on his fork to Cy Sylvester, and Cy told him it was a yaller eye. The next one was a Jacob's Cattle. Then Maxine began chasing down various kinds of baking beans, and Earl segregated 11 kinds. "It's an 11-course dinner," he said. He thought the juice was good, too, and approved the South West Bend custom of sopping it up with a hot biscuit. This went on until the entire company was staring at him, thinking the poor man had never seen food before—which may have been true. Then Doc told Earl to lay off and taper down a bit. "There's pie," said Doc.

A thoughtful attitude settled over Mr. Wilson, and he asked, "What kind?"

This is the famous occasion when Maxine put the smart-aleck from the city in his rightful place, and is often mentioned in these parts as a high historical event.

Doc said, "Oh, any kind you want—just name it, they'll bring it."

Earl didn't exactly accept this at face value, and as he finished wiping out his bean juice he meditated on all the kinds of pies that inventive housewives have manufactured since the law first went off this kind of amusement. Evidently it occurred to him to show Doc that he wasn't quite that gullible, and that he knew the pie situation was unduly elaborated for the effect on the visitor. He, too, knew a thing or so.

So Earl was ready and waiting when Maxine leaned her lovely complexion over his weather shoulder and asked, "What kind of pie will you have?"

Earl didn't want the snapper in this to come too soon. He wanted to show Doc that you couldn't kid a big writer from the big city. Earl said, "What kind of pie do you have?"

Maxine never batted an eye. "Why," she says, "did you have some special kind in mind?"

This was it! This thing was taking shape beautifully. Now Doc would see. Maxine had played right into his hands. Earl was ready. He had been thinking of the most unlikely kind of pie in the world, and now he was about to give Doc the works. "Any kind you want," Doc had said, "Just name it." Indeed! Earl would now name it. He articulated with extreme nicety, so everybody up and down the long table could see this demolishing denouement when it came.

Earl said, "I'll have a piece of cranberry and apricot cream pie."

Maxine promptly said, "Yes, sir, open or shut?"

So Earl had a piece of all the kinds there were, and then Maxine sold him one to take home. It was custard, about three inches thick, and they had a tin plate he could have to carry it on. Earl waved good-by to everybody when we left, and wished the furnace committee luck. He told them to let him know when they had another supper, because he never contributed 50¢ to a cause which gave him so much personal satisfaction. He said it was one of the few times in his life when he had donated to a fund and felt he got his money's worth. He held the pie in one hand and backed out the door waving with the other.

Doc and I put him on the next plane for New York, and we could see him through one of the little windows holding the pie on his knee and telling the stewardess all about it. He stifled a burp and waved at us as the plane moved out onto the runway. He was home and in bed, he said, at a good hour, but he never reported if his sleep was fitful. The athletic stomachs of good Maine people allow them to eat meals like that and then slumber as if nothing had happened. It always seemed strange that Earl ate so many beans and we never heard a report.

*You just can't
go wrong.*

ON THIS SUBJECT OF PIES THERE IS
much to be said yet. I was interested in a contest
recently conducted in Massachusetts to see who
could make the best pie. The contestants were
limited somewhat by one of the rules that said
the filling had to be Massachusetts cranberries
and Massachusetts apples together, which I think
is too bad. I think they could do better, but I don't
wish to start a fight over it.

I think you should know that I am quite some
pie maker myself. Ordinarily I don't have to make
them, as I support a capable wife for that purpose,
but when occasion demands I can make as good
a pie as anybody, contest or no contest. Last sum-

189

mer my family said they would like to go to salt water, which is a local euphemism for the seashore, and so they went down to salt water. I went down evenings before supper, and came back to my hill mornings after breakfast and we all managed to make out. Then one day I discovered that the Red Astrachan apples had achieved their majority, and lacking any loving hands to bake me a pie for dinner, I baked one myself.

It is not hard to bake a pie, and it is just as easy to bake a good one. I moved deftly about the kitchen, making no wasted motions, and shortly I slapped a couple of promising pies into the oven to see what heat would do for them—as if I didn't know. In due time they had been heated enough, and I was just about to inspect them when there came a knock to the back door. Hastily throwing off my ap'n, I opened up and found the dooryard full of tourists.

I imply nothing discourteous by calling them tourists. They were touring. They had two automobiles and were going together. I think they were from Illinois, but it may have been Michigan. All southern states are alike up here, and it may have been Dakota. They said they were passing through Maine, and having read some of the jocularities I dispense they had a desire to view the locale of so many whoppers. They asked me if I still had the hog with two heads, and I said that he had eaten one of his heads off, which is an ex-

190

pression, and they all laughed and had a good time. They seemed to be fine people, from Grandmother right down to a tyke in a playsuit made of seersucker and strawberry ice cream, and just as I finished meeting them all I came to with a start and said, "Oh, wait'll I take out my pies!"

So I rushed into the house and extracted my goodies, which steamed wonderfully and set up an advertising campaign. The folks watched through the screen and saw me do it, and they were impressed. Golden-browned and delightfully aromatic, the pies caught their fancy, and they were downright incredulous. "D-do you bake pies?" one of them asked.

"Oh, yes," I said, throwing the thing off as if it were nothing. True genius is ever modest at encomium. I could see this whole affair was wonderful publicity. If I had arranged the whole thing for its theatrical effect, it couldn't have been better. Somewhere out yonder a large family is waiting to recommend my new book just because they saw me bake some pies. I can see the reasonableness of this. Any good author can write a book, and a literary reputation based on that accomplishment is only what you'd expect. But when a man can lay down his typewriter and whip up a couple of nice-looking pies—there is a scholar indeed. His books must be good! I do not claim to understand this, I merely accept it because it appears to be so.

That evening I carried my two pies and a jar of

cream to my sojourning family, and they said my original thought had been sound. So, you see, I know something about pies.

Well, this woman won the Massachusetts pie contest—her name is Kay Mitchell and she lives in Wrentham—and a big chain grocery store immediately made a big thing out of the fact that she used their flour. They went on the radio, and bought space in the papers, and they said she used their flour and it was no wonder she won. They suggested anybody could tote home a bag of this flour, and immediately become a pie-making champion. There was almost nothing to it. Well, they're full of prunes, because in the New England *Homestead* they printed Mrs. Mitchell's prize-winning recipe, and the truth is out. It wasn't the flour she used at all.

It was chicken fat.

Her pastry mix includes one teaspoon of chicken fat. It isn't much, but it's the difference between anybody's pie and the pie of a champion. And I knew that all along. If those tourists had come a little sooner that pleasant morning, they'd have found me putting chicken fat in my pie crust, and they'd have known everything Kay Mitchell and I know. If you use chicken fat you can make a prize-winning pie out of any old flour. If you use chicken fat you can even make a pie out of Massachusetts cranberries and Massachus—but I wasn't going to say that. First, though, you have to have chicken fat.

We generally do. Since the price of poultry feed clambored into its present exhilarated position, I've grown field corn to aid my hens in their business. At times they've lived on it exclusively. It makes the eggs most yellow, and makes the hens very fat. Whenever we stew one for Sunday dinner, which is fairly often, we acquire another pail of chicken fat. We use it for everything. It is the magic ingredient, and in an era of prefabricated shortenings it seems to be the one you can purchase the least of. A chain store, I suppose, wouldn't know about it.

So remember the chicken fat! And while Mrs. Mitchell is being memorialized because she uses somebody's special blend of bleached, rarefied, emulsicated, fortituted, splenderized and scarifacted flour, don't be misled. My books may not be so good, but they sell well—and I never worry whose flour I use. Just drop in some chicken fat when you bake a pie, and you'll swear I'm the greatest author of all time.

❀ ❀ ❀

Glad to get back
to work.

OUR MODERN AGE ISN'T ALWAYS
equal to improving its time, and artificial methods
of finding something to do have proved a boon.
The old-timers had no such requirements, and
could fill their days with activity just by taking
advantage of what they had. Like Uncle Ivory.

He lives up the road a piece, and he demonstrated a while back that attitude is an important
factor. He had finished stripping a row of milkers
and was carrying two pails to the strainer when
his foot touched a damp place where the temperature of our modest weather had skimmed things
over with a little ice. The hired man heard a
swoosh and a whumpf, and saw about seventeen
of the farm's twenty-three cats racing to the scene
with their tongues hanging out. Then he heard the
slup-slup of the lapping cats, and after a search he
located Uncle Ivory at the far end of the tie-up.
Uncle Ivory didn't know he was at the far end of
the tie-up, he thought he had remained where he
fell. The momentum had exceeded his anticipation,
however, and he had coasted in under a bench
with one pail on over his head. The other pail
hasn't been found yet.

Uncle Ivory was not greatly upset over this, so
to speak, because he had been telling the hired
boy to put sand on that spot for the past two

194

weeks, and felt his prophecy had come to an exemplary fruition. Uncle Ivory spent several minutes saying I-told-you-so, pushing cats away at the same time, and shortly he became attentive again to his chores and fell silent.

But when he went to climb up in the mow and pitch down a little hay, the sixth rung of the ladder came loose in his hands and astonished him. He had also been telling the boy to fix that rung for quite some time, and as he picked himself up from the barn floor he called this to the attention of the boy in such a fashion that people all up and down the road heard him. He continued to mention this dereliction of duty on the part of the boy, off and on, all during supper, and said that maybe the next time he opened his head to speak there would be somebody who would pay attention. He hoped. He said it was possible to hire somebody to do everything else but the thinking, and he felt as long as they left that all up to him, they should be more diligent in carrying out the results of his thoughts. He was starting to go to bed, without relaxing the thread of his discourse, when he happened to think he hadn't watered the bull, so he put his boots on again and went out to water the bull.

As he was stepping into the barn the wind blew the door shut on his heels and tripped him over the threshold, and then the pump handle lashed back and caught him under the chin—but these things didn't bother him any. Also, the bail pulled off one side of the bucket and filled one of his boots with nice cold well water. But he's used to little things like that as a consequence of his duties, so he soon had another pail of water before the bull, and the bull was sucking away and was openly grateful to have his drink after he had come to suppose Uncle Ivory had forgotten him for the night. Uncle Ivory, glad he hadn't really forgotten after all, permitted a deep sense of satisfaction to well up in his breast, and to display his generosity and affection to all of God's creatures, he reached over and scratched Bonnie Maggie's Elm'aple Safeguard II lovingly between the horns and gave him a soft pat of affection. This pleased the bull a great deal, and to show that this kindly feeling was reciprocated, he lifted his head suddenly from the bucket in much the same way the back piazza would lift if somebody set off a bomb under it. Uncle Ivory had to step back quickly or be killed.

When he did, he stepped on the blade of a hoe that was lying close by, and the handle flew up and cuffed Uncle Ivory on the ear. It seems the hoe had been lying across a snatch of hay on which a cat had stretched out asleep, and the action catapulted the cat. She sailed up into the haymow and came down athwart a broody hen who had gone up there to await a certain day two weeks come Tuesday. It is presumed that the din was notable, but Uncle Ivory had somehow got his head in the bull's water pail, and the bull was now trying to drink some more. The more Uncle Ivory, dazed to some extent, tried to pull out of the bucket, the thirstier the bull became, and for a short time things were nip and tuck. But Uncle Ivory got loose, all right, and sat awhile on an apple crate to catch his breath. Just as he was catching, the apple crate collapsed.

Then Uncle Ivory kicked the apple crate into a hayrack body that had been hoisted up into the scaffling mow and went into the house without putting off any lights, shutting any doors, or looking either to the right or to the left.

He said he had enough. He said he was through. He said farming was more than he could stand another second. He said the place was for sale, terms reasonable. He said if he could find a half-wit would take it, he'd give the thing away. He spoke for quite some time in this vein, and then went to bed, stubbing his big toe forcefully on the third step of the front stairs, thus discovering that he had already removed his boots down in the kitchen.

I believe I have neglected to mention that Uncle Ivory was seventy-nine years of age last August 23rd.

He got up the next morning and took breakfast, but made no effort to join in the day's work. He sat in a big chair by the window and watched

197

the hired boy and the hired man come and go. He saw the truck drive off with the cans of milk, and he sat right there until dinnertime. After dinner he sat there until supper, and after supper he sat there until bedtime. Then he went to bed. It certainly looked as if Uncle Ivory had retired.

The next morning he arose at 4.30 and milked the cows all by himself. He did all the barn work, took the milk to town, and was home for breakfast at 7.30. He ate a large meal, including pie, and got up from the table and went out and did a day's work. The only remark he has made since which could be construed as comment on his day of leisure was to the effect that he didn't understand how so many people can sit around all the time and never do anything but sit around. "Drive me batty," he said. "I couldn't do it. I got to have something to do. I hate to have time hanging on my hands. There's plenty to do without looking for it, and I just can't sit around and think about it."

❦ ❦ ❦

*It was good while
it lasted.*

EVERY TIME I GO FISHING I HAVE to listen to learned dissertations from veteran anglers about which flies will take fish and which

198

won't. Between times I read it again in one of the 10,000 books that purports to be the authoritative work. But I've decided I know as much about it as anybody. When I try to say so, I get pish-toshed at a great rate, so all I can do is tell about Pinocchio. If Pinocchio doesn't prove something, I don't know what it is.

Years ago they had a grim-looking fellow for State Policeman on Route One. He had a heart of gold but an ingrown determination not to let anybody know it. He was popular with local folks, but could scare the weasel juice out of a tourist in a manner beyond belief. He looked like a thunderstorm riding a motorcycle, and after he had stopped an out-of-state car for cutting in on a hill, he would saunter over, adjust the wrath of God on his tanned countenance, hoist one foot akimbo, and in the sweetest tones would say, "Good awftanoon, and welcome most cordially to the beauties and pleasures of the Pine Tree State!" While he was on Route One he had respect from everybody who toured it, and is still remembered by many offenders as the nicest guy who ever arrested them. His name was, and still is, Rosswell C. Hamilton, but everybody called him Razz and he didn't mind. He had a smash-up on his motorcycle and later moved over to the motor vehicle registry with a bad back. While he was a Maine State Police trooper his homecomings were erratic, and his wife sought some way to amuse herself at home.

She took to tying flies and got to be a dabster at it, and tied some of the best I've ever seen. She called herself the Royal River Fly Company, and the dining room table was the factory. While Razz was out making tourists comfortable she would fit feathers and hooks together, and sometimes make more money than he did. When he came home she'd jump up and break some eggs in the pan, and that's the way it was.

Razz didn't know one fly from another, and never became a manufacturing expert, but while he was waiting for dinner he'd sit at the little vise and fool around. His wife tried to get him interested in standard patterns, where the money lay, but Razz was an individualist, thank goodness, and he kept the whole countryside amused at his inventions. The infinite variety available to an experimental fly maker is beyond belief, and Razz pumped with both feet and kept all the stops out.

He never sold any of his own concoctions, but gave them to friends to amuse them. One day he gave me one. I had a spasm of hysterics, because it belied every tradition of the art, but Razz enjoyed cheering people up and my hilarity moved him not. This one had no connection with established fact, and combined all known colors in such a way that while each was dominant none

200

was subjugated. The junglecock was on backwards, a little to loo'ard of the tail, and I had to look twice to see which end was eyed. Razz had tied it while his wife was frying a mess of smelts, and in that salubrious atmosphere he had let himself go. It was called, he said, Pinocchio. Just at that time Walt Disney had released his cartoon by that name and Pinocchio was a household word. I thanked Razz, snagged the fly into my hat, and fought off the starlings while he hopped on his motorcycle and took after a sedan from Ohio.

Anglers will want me to include all the details. The fly in my hat enhanced my notoriety about town. People made yodels at me from across the street. Others came across to ask me if I knew it was there. The hardware store gave me a free can of bug-death and a leaflet on tomato worms. One fellow who went back and forth to the post office frequently got a pair of sun glasses, and he'd whip them out when he saw me and complain because I was spoiling his eyesight. Somebody said Fred Gamache's wife's new baby was marked with colored stripes. The boys at the town offices started a petition asking me to pose as a model for a Christmas tree in the town park, but they changed it so it just said to keep off the street between ten and two.

The next day Pat Sawyer and I went over to Sebago Lake to get a salmon apiece for Fourth of July dinner, and I still had Pinocchio in my hat when he came to pick me up. He let out a whoop and pulled down the sun visor over his windshield. He guessed it was an Italian Sunset or the Chicago Fire, and said it was nothing I should intrude into the life of a pious and earnest angler who had never done me any harm, but whose conduct had been rectitude itself and whose devotion to steadfast principles was common knowledge. He told me to hide it under a bushel. I pretended a great hurt at his levity and told him never to laugh at a fly until he had seen what it would do. Those were my very words, and I want all anglers to take due notice. I said, "Never make fun of a fly until it has been under water."

Then we went fishing. As an experienced angler I had not, up to that moment, intended to put Pinocchio in the water. He was a hat-fly only. Even Razz Hamilton wouldn't have thought of fishing with the thing. It was to make girls giggle as they went by, or to make strong men find a place to sit down and pant, but it was not for fishing. Any angler would be more subtle than that. But Pat overdid a little, and all the way to the lake he kept suggesting cures for color-blindness, and making remarks about my poor wife and what she puts up with. We were fitting the lunch buckets under the thwarts of the boat and he was still going strong. He said anybody who would tie a thing like that was a fine thing to have on

202

the State Police, and he probably couldn't tell his elbow from a hole in the ground, or words to that effect. Quite an audience gathered at the boat landing, because Pat is good when he gets going.

So the natural thing for me to do was fit Pinocchio to my leader, which I did with great show. I whipped him in the air a few times and it looked like the rainbow in the mists of Niagara. Pat shielded his eyes and made a great honking, as if a flock of Canada Geese were going over, and all the people on the landing laughed.

Now every word is absolute truth, but even if I lied it would still be a good story. Just as we got out of the cove into the big lake, Pat sewed on a minnow and went into his customary explanation of why he catches more and bigger ones than anybody else. It is because he uses featherstitching. Other people just sew, but Pat has studied salmon and knows they are fussy. Plain sewing is no good. He spit on his minnow, hove it overboard, and I dropped Pinocchio on the other side of the boat. "Well," said Pat. "Good luck!"

At that precise moment a salmon jumped four feet into the azure sky, shook his tail so you could hear the scales rub together, and went below with Pinocchio. I set the hook with expert touch, kicked the net closer with my foot, and began to play with the fish as is my joyful wont. I have many times bragged that never once have I lost a fish that was fairly hooked. Slowly, carefully, expertly

I anticipated every move, and the salmon was as good as baked before I slipped the net around him and relaxed the line.

Pat is coolness himself when he hooks a fish, but when I hook one he goes all to pieces. He reels in his own line so he won't foul me, and then stands up and shouts encouragement and advice at the top of his lungs. People come out of cottages all up and down the lake to see if a boat has capsized and forty are drowning. Every time my salmon broke water he looked as if he had the flags of all nations in his mouth, and a streak of fire to boot. Pat yelped and whooped, and in due time we boated a very nice *Salmo Sebago,* or Maine landlocked salmon.

Pat said, "The damned fool took Pinocchio!"

With great calm I said, "Yes. I plan always to use a fly fish will take. I have experimented for years, and find that's a good rule. I have tried to say as much in the presence of many anglers, but all I get is the old ho-ho, what do you know about it, and this grieves me until with patient submission I keep silent. I would not [I said] waste my time on something such as you are using, particularly if I was serious about salmon for Fourth of July this year."

Pat told me to go to hell.

I added that if he had eyes to see, my standing as an angler was now well established, and if he had the kindness to acknowledge it I would

204

forget all the jeers he had made at my Pinocchio. While I was saying this, of course, I believed deep down that this salmon was crazy, and that his taking Pinocchio was merely a miracle so I could get even with Pat. This was not so, however. Before Pat got his minnow overboard again I had a second salmon on my line—much bigger than the first. I boated him neatly, commenting on my dexterity as I went along so Pat would be sure to notice the fine points of my agility and know-how. Then I caught my third salmon on Pinocchio before Pat was through admiring the second.

Three is the lawful limit on Sebago, so in theory I was all done fishing for the day. Pat threw down his own rod, scrambled the length of the boat and snarled, "You can't break the law when I'm with you, gimme that rod!"

In the next half hour Pat hooked five salmon, but he boated only two of them. Pat was in no condition to exercise his customary skill. Pinocchio's strange success unnerved him, and he sat there gibbering and frothing at the mouth. He was a mess. Babbling like a babe, incoherent—he did the wrong things and lost three nice salmon that, I'm sure, a man of my calm disposition would easily have landed. It might be that little things I said while he was fishing contributed to his state of mind, but I know I said nothing intentionally designed to upset him. The fifth one came aboard, and Pat said, "Take me home, I've had enough."

He laid back and grinned a fond, foolish, satisfied smirk, his face bemused and bewildered.

On the way in he said, "We've got a killer! That cop is a genius! All these years, thousands upon thousands of dollars spent for gray ghosts, green ghosts, Arnold specials, Barnes specials—and none of them any good. Whango! Along comes Pinocchio! We've got to keep quiet about this, or next Sunday they'll clean the lake out."

But it was Pat who gave it away. We got ashore and a couple of wardens checked our catch. All day they had been checking, and nobody had caught a thing. At 5.30 they checked with other places around the lake, and not a salmon had come ashore since daybreak. There we were with five, and Pat apologetically offered that he had hooked three others but lost them. Nobody believed him. People crowded around ten deep to see our fish, but nobody believed him.

Then some unhappy angler wearing fifteen hundred dollars worth of L. L. Bean gear inquired what we took them on. This is traditional fishing ritual. What you catch is the least of the story—most important is what you took them on. On this day, with hundreds of skunked boats, the question had electric significance.

Pat drew himself up to twice his height, appropriated all the glory that should have been mine, and with clear and concise diction he announced, "We used Pinocchio!"

Silence, and then somebody gasped, "Pinocchio!"

The word ran around the landing. "Pinocchio!"

"Eyup," Pat said. "Pinocchio."

Inasmuch as none of the assembly had ever heard of Pinocchio, their reaction was interesting. They indicated to a man that while it would never have occurred to them to use Pinocchio, they could see how wise it would have been. So silly not to have thought of it. You'd have sworn each of them had dozens of Pinocchios in his box. This was just being compounded nicely when one of the wardens—and wardens are an honest lot—spoiled it by saying, "And what is Pinocchio?"

"Pinocchio," I said, ". . . Pinocchio is a salmon fly designed after years of exhaustive research, making use of the corneal rectilinity of the salmonic optic nerve. The deductions are highly technical, but they consist mostly of employing a color combination which makes an odor. The salmon strikes on account of the smell." I lowered my hat and pointed to Pinocchio and the group shielded their eyes and looked and we could see they were impressed. The next morning the Portland paper said Sebago fishing was unaccountably poor, but that one party had miraculously taken five beautiful salmon on the Royal River Pinocchio —now considered the leading salmon fly.

That afternoon Officer Hamilton dragged his motorcycle to a stop in my dooryard. A strange and hunted look was in his eye, and he grabbed me by the shoulders and yelled, "For God's sake —have you still got Pinocchio?"

I said that I certainly had.

Razz sighed with relief and said, "Then gimme it quick—we got orders for 1,500 gross of Pinocchios, and I don't remember what it looked like."

With the one and only Pinocchio before her, Razz's wife would be able to fill the orders, and while Razz never exhibited any lush sentiment towards me at other times, I thought that morning he was going to sweep me into his arms and give me a great big wet kiss. He drove off one-handed, clutching the valuable pattern in the other. They said his wife was waiting for him on the front steps. During the next few weeks she tied countless Pinocchios. They were in every tackle shop in the state, and anglers bought them six at a time. Fishermen's hats looked like artists' palettes, and the waters of Sebago were whipped to a froth with Pinocchios. People forgot all about Walt Disney, and when somebody asked, "Have you seen Pinocchio?" he wasn't talking about any old moving picture.

But the sad and disturbing fact is that Pinocchio never took another fish. There is no record of any kind that Pinocchio ever enticed again. Even now, years afterward, when nothing else seems to work, fishermen will dig down in their tackle boxes and bring him out, but he won't work either. As far as I know those five fish at Sebago are the only fish ever caught with Pinocchio.

Pinocchio is a dud. Once Pat went up to Rainbow Lake and found everybody sitting around moping. In two weeks nobody had seen a fish. Pat arose at supper and said he invited everybody to a trout breakfast. He said, "I shall arise at daybreak, and with Pinocchio I shall catch enough for everybody." Pat arose at daybreak, and went out with Pinocchio, but he came in at breakfast and ate ham and eggs with the rest of them. He stayed a week and never saw a fish.

So now when I go fishing and have to listen to all this conversation about which fly will do what, and how a dark Montreal is preferred to a bucktail Silver Doctor—I sit back and wait and at a convenient time I tell about Pinocchio. I think Pinocchio tells the whole story, from A to Z. You can get to be a purist, and multitudes will listen with devoted attention. It makes good talk, and you can expound until the cows come home. But Pinocchio is a perennial sour note, and he says that the best time to catch fish is when they're biting. In fact, he says when they're biting, you can catch them best of all.

VOLTAIRE WAS WEALTHY
from his pen, and others who wrote in former
times did rather well. Men turned from the hurly-
burly of trading and trafficking and meditated
on affairs and produced deathless works. They
were encouraged to do so by the grateful public
they served.

In ancient days the poet and author were highly
esteemed. People considered their judgments as

211

they conducted political affairs. Many ancient literary figures were elevated to high office and their wisdom aided decorum and economy. The place of honor at the feast was reserved for the minstrel, and he was rewarded both materially and with the adulation of a cultured audience.

Patronage went arm in arm with creative work, and the man whose genius deserved support was sure to find it. What would we have of the classic forms and contents if popes, princes and potentates had neglected to foster the arts and support the hungry artists?

It is not now as it hath bean of yore. Today a fellow who tries to live by the gentle, winged word is the victim of every hostile device, and his spirit perishes from oppression and depression. Just as he settles himself into a cordial frame of mind, and is about to produce an imperishable work, some government man comes to ask him how much money he will earn in the year ahead. This is a severe thing to have happen at that crucial time. How would he know? With the vapors of artistry about his shoulders like a muse's shawl, the author doesn't know, and if he's a good author he doesn't care. The spirit that weighs and measures humanity is above a mercenary premise.

It's nice to have enough to live on, and it's nice to have a million dollars—but the true writer writes the same in either condition, and doesn't write so well if he stops to think about it. But the government man doesn't care if literature survives or perishes, and he tells the author he must estimate his income. The great work is thus delayed, and while it is delayed some critic rises to inquire why American letters are in such a low state. The graphic arts, he argues, have perfected every facility to carry the writer's thoughts and stories to every hamlet and every home. Why, he repeats, is there so little good writing? The world, he says, is hungry for quality—why is there so much crap?

The author is meantime thinking that if they make jelly and sell enough at 35¢ the jar they might possibly take in $125 in August. This means $450 is due and payable on March 15th, and the author doesn't have it. He got his last royalty check for $7.50 in November, and won't get another until May—if he gets one. By this time any brave literary thoughts have been dispelled, and the imperishable work is deader than John of Gaunt. The world continues to starve for something worth reading, and the author considers joining a crew to cup pulpwood—where his taxes will be withheld at source, his social security and unemployment insurance will be deducted for him, and his immediate acquaintances wouldn't know John Greenleaf Whittier from the Duke of Burgundy.

Do not minimize the effect modern times have on writing and writers. Patronage is gone. Even Voltaire would write cultch and twiddle today, because he'd be in the higher tax brackets. You can't whistle with your mouth full of crackers, and you can't turn from a government form and do a decent ditty. Some things are contrary to nature. Esteem and respect for the creative spirit are unpopular, and nobody cares. A piece I wrote a short time ago was plagiarized by the Congressional Record, printed in full without permission at the request of some Congressman I never heard from. Presumably he placed it on record because it would please the people, and impart some gladness in essential places. My taxes are just as high as if I never thus entranced the admiring public, but a plumber who fixes a public sink gets an appropriation. I didn't get so much as a thank-you from the Public Printer. But Bobby Burns was appointed exciseman in his day and did rather well at it. John Milton was a state secretary. Cicero was consul; Octavianus himself assured Vergil of his lands. Even Sophocles was elected a general when he wasn't even a candidate. But when I wrote to Senator Brewster and said I would like to be Commissioner of the Penobscot Boom, he neglected to do anything about it.

I have no objection to paying taxes or taking part in any public program where I can help. But such service should be as an honor, not as a penalty, and then I could write well too. I have no promise of pension or patronage—not even the boon of privacy with my creative thoughts. If I could afford it I would gladly pay the entire costs of government myself, and spare all the other people that bother. The other people, some of whom can afford it, read my efforts in the Congressional Record and make no offer to reward me. They could aid the course of literature by allowing me to dwell undisturbed among my untrodden ways without worrying about the state of the union. But will they?

In consequence of affairs as they are, I must therefore ask my readers not to recommend this work too highly, to be cautious in promoting it, and to try and keep the sales down as much as possible. I am trying to live within my deductions and thus keep a cool head for my deathless thoughts. The minute I find I've got to pay taxes, and no chance of even a garland bestowed by the Library of Congress, I go all to pieces, and dealing with the quintuplicate details of mercenary government ruins me for months. I'm not worth a tinker's darn. Some days I can't lay one word on another and do it straight, just because a hungry administration treads me down and my sensitive spirit sulks.

So please don't noise it about that this book is now for sale. I produced it only because my publisher wants me to keep my name before the public, and he feels the Congressional Record is not a suitable medium for unqualified fame. Perhaps he is right.

I might add, in conclusion, that we do have a high quality jelly during August and September, and also maple syrup in season. I used to do these country chores so I could write about them and earn some money. But now I continue to do them as relaxation from the disturbing life of a modern author. I enter the net loss on my annual form as "Occupational Therapy."